Love Skills

Linda De Villers, Ph.D.

Love

Skills

More Fun
than
You've Ever Had
with Sex,
Intimacy and Communication

Impact Publishers®
SAN LUIS OBISPO, CALIFORNIA 93406

Impact Publishers and colophon are registered trademarks of Impact Publishers, Inc.

ATTENTION ORGANIZATIONS AND CORPORATIONS:
This book is available at quantity discounts on bulk purchases for educational, business, or sales promotional use. For further information, please contact Impact Publishers, P.O. Box 1094, San Luis Obispo, CA 93406 (Phone: 1-800-246-7228).

Library of Congress Cataloging-in-Publication Data
De Villers, Linda.
    Love skills : more fun than you've ever had with sex, intimacy and communication / Linda De Villers
        p.   cm.
    Includes bibliographical references and index.
    ISBN 0-915166-93-3 (alk. paper)
    1. Sex.   2. Man-woman relationships.   I. Title.
HQ21.D46   1996
306.7----dc20   96-34932
                                                CIP

Printed in the United States of America on acid-free paper
Cover design by Sharon Schnare, San Luis Obispo, California

Published by **Impact 🕮 Publishers**®
POST OFFICE BOX 1094
SAN LUIS OBISPO, CALIFORNIA 93406

Contents

Dedication

To my parents,
Mary and Bruce,
whose love, wisdom and role-modeling
gave me roots, vision and wings.

Acknowledgements

I am truly grateful to so many people. Many directly contributed to the realization of this book. Many others, whose paths have crossed mine at one time or another, have enriched my life in all ways possible. They have made me the person I am and the creation of this book possible.

I bless my wonderful and loyal friends, a number of whom are also my truly exceptional and outstanding teaching colleagues. I also cherish my terrific professional friends in the Society for the Scientific Study of Sexuality, AASECT and the Los Angeles County Psychological Association. They have all given me the emotional and intellectual nourishment needed to be inspired, to thrive and to persevere.

I'd like to thank the thousands of students, clients and seminar participants who have shared their lives with me and from whom I have learned so much. All those who so generously volunteered assistance at various stages along the way deserve a special thanks (in alphabetical order): Judy Cleaveland, Debbie Colwell, Rachel Fintzy, Jan Fogelman, Julie Fulkerson, Joanne Galbreath, Stacey Lehrman, Lynda Moore, Janice Sherbourne, Cathy Snow and Robert Vargas.

I bless my mother for her constant love, her strength and her unwavering support and faith in me throughout my life. Early on, she planted the seeds of inspiration with her periodic comment: "I just know you're going to write a book some day." I thank all the members of my family for being such great people. My brother, Ken, deserves special acknowledgment for his careful comments on early drafts. The loving memory of my father, a wonderful person and role model, is also with me.

I thank Dennis James for coming into my life just when I needed him and for offering me so much love and support. My deepest appreciation goes to Bob Alberti of Impact Publishers. He has been consistently conscientious, gracious, helpful and reasonable. I truly thank him for giving me this opportunity to provide readers with the insights and helpful suggestions I've garnered over the years through my teaching, private work with clients and seminar leading.

Last, but definitely not least, I want to thank Jean Marie Stine. She has seen me through this project from its inception to its conclusion, providing brilliant editorial assistance. She has been a wonderful friend, an intellectual soulmate, and a mentor. I loved all that we shared, both professionally and personally. It was a great experience!

— *Linda De Villers*

LOVE SKILLS
"More fun than you've ever had"

"I never dreamed how much fun sex could be. We used to approach it as a physical work kind of thing. Trying to push and pull the right levers and things. That seemed difficult enough. Now it's easy, because we've learned to make sex fun and keep it fun."

(Donna, 29)

"I wish I had told my husband what turns me on sexually a long time ago. It would have saved us from a lot of bad feelings and a lot of heartache…" (Monica, 36)

"I'm at the point sexually in my relationship that I'm bored with the same old stuff. I'd like to try new things." (Gary, 24)

"I don't know if I want to tell him that 'I miss you kissing all over my back.' Touching in my relationship is limited to nothing but the necessary areas." (Faye, 40)

"Sex is supposed to be simple, but it isn't. I really wish we could get a tutorial of some sort so that we could learn how to have a really rich and nourishing sex life. It would add a lot to our relationship."

(Adam, 33)

I f sex isn't fun, it isn't anything.
    Think about it. What do you want from a sexually
intimate relationship?

If you're like most people, your list probably contains at
least some of the following:

- Easy, comfortable intimacy
- Deep passion
- Hot lovemaking
- Affirmation of yourself as a sexually desirable person
- Verbal expression of your partner's love and lust
- Variety and creativity
- Sexually daring moments

Sounds like fun, doesn't it? And that's exactly what this
book is about — having as much *fun* as is possible with the
intimacy, communication and sex in your relationship.

The *Love Skills* approach to bringing playfulness,
excitement and variety into your erotic encounters asks you
to make a sacrifice: *You have to give up the myth that "great sex
is natural."*

Knowing what your lover likes best and blending into
an erotic symphony together doesn't "just come naturally."
Developing skills in communication, intimacy and sexual
contact is one of the biggest challenges couples face.

What's usually lacking is not the will — but the way.
The right way to communicate, to be intimate, to blend into
a larger, more exciting sexual whole.

We're all born with the basic "hardware" needed to
express our sexuality, but the "software" program — how to
make the most of it and how to communicate with each other
about it — is learned.

The idea that "love will conquer all" is well-intended but
naive; it simply doesn't work that way when it comes to
relating to lovers. As soon as you start a new relationship,

you discover how little you know about making sex, communication and intimacy work.

Most of us lack one or more of the all-vital skills of love and, when sexually intimate relationships go wrong, that lack is often the missing link.

It's not surprising, nor is it our fault. We live in a culture that has done very little to encourage us to learn about or to be comfortable communicating about sex.

But it's never too late — especially if you can have fun in the process.

What Are the Love Skills?

In the following chapters, you'll find a playful, fun approach to learning "everything you need to know" to heal up, maintain and deepen an intimate relationship.

It all starts with learning those *Love Skills* you've been lacking. That isn't hard. You only need four skills to create sexual intimacy and communication. And they are all very easy to learn. The four Love Skills are:

- *LoveTalk* — the ability to communicate about sexual matters, both out of and in bed.
- *BodyLove* — the ability to love, accept and enjoy your body and that of your lover.
- *LoveTouch* — the ability to give and receive affirmation through the senses alone.
- *LovePlay* — the ability to be creative, playful — and occasionally sexually naughty — in or out of bed.

What Can You Expect from this Book?

In developing these four skills and this book, I've drawn from many years of professional experience with clients and workshop participants, from more than fifteen years teaching graduate courses in human sexuality, and from my own personal experience. (Believe it or not, psychologists make love too!) The *Love Skills* program works because it gives lovers a systematic program for change, based on breakthrough scientific understandings of relationships and what makes them sizzle. But don't let the "scientific" part scare you.

These ideas aren't mere theory — although they are based on a sound, scientific, coherent perspective — they've worked for hundreds of people just like you.

This is not another traditional "cookbook" sex manual. Nor is it a book about how to find love, or the nature of love, or the meaning of love. The purpose of this book is very specific: *to add sugar, spice, and sizzle to your committed love relationship.*

Love Skills leads you through an easy, step-by-step approach to blending sex, intimacy *and* communication skills. The process can liberate you to more fully enjoy and continually deepen the physical and emotional aspect of your sexuality and your love relationship.

As you progress through these gradual, easy-to-learn *Love Skills*, you'll find yourself communicating better, savoring each other more thoroughly, becoming more accepting of yourselves and each other, and making love in more playful and daring ways than you can imagine.

Along the way, you'll be provided with the specific insights, strategies and techniques needed to build and sustain passionate, romantic sexual intimacy into your love life.

To make your journey more enjoyable, the book is filled with the voices of real people just like you and your lover, who have experienced the same kinds of sexual challenges you face, and who frankly share their own candid stories, thoughts and reactions on love, sex, intimacy, communication and the rest.

These quotations are drawn from personal interviews and confidential surveys I've conducted with thousands of workshop participants, clients and students — and they were generous enough to share with me — over the years. You're sure to find their comments helpful, thought-provoking and insightful.

(Be warned, they are also uninhibited and quite earthy on occasion. But becoming comfortable with talking about love in frank, sexual terms is one of the skills this book teaches.)

Who Will Read this Book?

Love Skills is for anyone, couple or individual, male or female, straight, gay, bi (or anywhere between!) who:

- Wants a more exciting love life
- Is experiencing conflicts with a lover over sex and sexual issues
- Is having trouble with sexual communication
- Isn't getting what she wants from her lover
- Feels sexually stifled by routine
- Feels he isn't fully pleasing his lover
- Is concerned over a significant decrease in desire, frequency or satisfaction
- Wants to experiment with more exciting love play but doesn't know where or how to start
- Has become so frustrated with the present state of lovemaking that she is contemplating an affair
- Seeks to learn more about sex, love, relationships, communication and intimacy
- Is a therapist or member of the clergy counseling couples in committed relationships.

How Is the Book Organized?

Each of the next four sections is designed to make acquiring one of the four Love Skills easy and fun, and to bring you and your lover closer together while doing it.

Love Skill #1 — *LoveTalk* — shows you what a powerful tool open communication — about sex, love and intimate feelings — can be in creating a healthy loving relationship. It introduces you to the insights and delights that result from becoming comfortable using intimate and sexual language. You'll learn to use "Vertical" (out-of-bed) LoveTalk to discuss everything from sexual preferences to long-standing sexual disagreements. And you'll discover how to use "Horizontal" (in-bed) LoveTalk to sizzle during amorous encounters.

Love Skill #2 — *BodyLove* — will help liberate you from the inhibitions, dissatisfactions and sense of inadequacy we all feel about our bodies. You'll learn how to abandon yourself fully to the enjoyment of your own and your lover's sexuality. And you'll discover how to enhance your sense of your body's sexiness so that you approach each erotic encounter confident of your own strong physical appeal to your lover.

Love Skill #3 — *LoveTouch* — takes you from talk to the first step in creating physical intimacy — touching and being touched. It will lead you safely through a minefield of prohibitions that prevent most of us from fully surrendering to the nourishing pleasures of stroking, fondling, caressing. It will open your heart to the affection and intimacy that touch can express. Then it will slowly introduce you to the sensual pleasures of caressing and being caressed. And it will take you beyond to the sexual delights of touch, which stoke the fires of passion and erotic desire.

Love Skill #4 — *LovePlay* — is a provocative journey into expanding sexual horizons. You'll discover the importance, delights and rewards of being sexually playful and creative. You'll be presented with a cornucopia of suggestions — drawn from those that other couples have found added spice to their love lives. And you'll take a "baby steps" approach — stopping any time either of you feels the least bit uncomfortable — to expanding your sexual repertoire into activities you've thought were "daring," "off-beat," even a bit "naughty" until now.

When you have finished this book, you will have had an exciting adventure in loving. You'll also have discovered how to create a passionate, continually deepening relationship while having more fun than you ever thought possible with sex, communication and intimacy.

By the way, if you should run across material in this book that causes you to say to yourself, "Hmmmm, I don't think I could do that... it feels uncomfortable (awkward, anxious,...), don't judge yourself. The material in *Love Skills* is drawn from solid psychological principles and extensive research in human sexuality. Nevertheless, since it has been written for a wide audience, the ideas presented here won't fit all readers equally. So if you or your lover experience any discomfort, try one of these approaches:

• *Let the activity help you grow.* Take a deep breath and go for it, if the discomfort is relatively minor, and if your lover agrees.

• *Turn to "Love Skills Tips for Anxious Moments"* (page 199). You'll find there a number of helpful suggestions for dealing with your discomfort.

• *Skip it.* Obviously, I hope you'll want to *try* the suggestions I've made in the chapters that follow. But if you find any that just don't seem to work for you — for whatever reason — pass them by. You'll still get a lot out of your reading of *Love Skills*.

Love Skill One:
Love Talk

1

SEX-CESSFUL LOVETALK
"The more you know, the more you can do"

"Talking sexy makes having sex a lot more enjoyable, pleasurable and exciting... knowing what excites him excites me even more."
(Leanne, 26)

"Talking about sex can be very romantic because it allows for you and your lover to know what one another likes, enhances your sex life, and brings you closer." (Beverly, 50)

"Open sexual communication enables each lover to know the other even more. The more you know the more you can do for each other or understand likes/dislikes, etc." (Barry, 37)

"Talking about sex with my husband has improved my sex life tremendously. I can tell him what I would like for him to do to increase my pleasure. I know things to say to him to heighten his passion." (Robin, 41)

"In the beginning of my current relationship, we didn't talk about sex as openly as we do now. It could be frustrating because it became a guessing game." (Natasha, 29)

The first step toward injecting more fun into your lovelife and steaming up your amorous encounters — in or out of bed — is LoveTalk. Talking about sex is a Love Skill all its own — a vital aspect of establishing and maintaining a positive erotic connection with your lover. *Your lover cannot read your mind!* Unless you're able to discuss your erotic likes and dislikes openly, your lover can't know what they are — or what would turn you on next while making love. To kindle a sex-cessful relationship, the two of you must feel free to talk — comfortably, clearly and honestly — about sex.

Before you can become fully comfortable with your body, with touching each other or with sex play, you have to be able to engage comfortably in two LoveTalk formats, "vertical" and "horizontal."

Vertical LoveTalk takes place out of bed — when you're not intimately involved.

Horizontal LoveTalk occurs in bed — in the midst of sexual activity.

What's So Good About LoveTalk?

Your ability to engage in honest and uninhibited LoveTalk (both vertical and horizontal) has many benefits:

LoveTalk gives you a chance to learn more about each other sexually. When you can express yourself, you're far more able to give and receive what really turns you on and maximize your erotic pleasure.

LoveTalk feedback relieves the anxiety of "second guessing" what your lover wants and whether he or she is actually satisfied.

LoveTalk reduces sexual misunderstandings that can trigger feelings of resentment and turn off one or both of you.

LoveTalk adds excitement to your love life and reduces boredom as you find yourselves constantly devising new ways to be erotic together.

LoveTalk builds a new sense of intimacy that comes from sharing your own unique erotic vocabulary, intimate knowledge of your lover's turn-ons and offs, and sharing each other's most "secret" sexual fantasies.

Flirtatious or erotic LoveTalk is a terrific means of building anticipation and desire. It's fun, creative and sexy!

What Inhibits LoveTalk? Social Myths

A number of widely held — but wrong — beliefs and social attitudes make it very difficult for most of us to talk openly about sexual matters. Here are a few of the mistaken ideas:

"Sex is natural; talking about it is a waste of time." You'll have a hard time convincing the television, publishing and motion picture industries of this argument! Healthy people always have a natural curiosity about sex, and talking about it holds almost everybody's interest and attention.

It is often men who hold the notion that "sex is natural so there's nothing to talk about." When you buy into this, however, and fail to discuss your erotic turn-ons and turn-offs with your lover, there's no way you can receive or give all the pleasure you want from sex. If you don't know your lover's wants, you are making love to her by rote — and not as an individual with specific needs and turn-ons just like you. (Not surprisingly, the most frequent sexual complaint of women is that men are too "mechanical" in their lovemaking.)

"It's unromantic to talk about sex." This notion takes some specific twists and turns depending on your gender. Women often fall into the trap of believing that, "If he loved me, he'd know what to do." That's certainly the way books, movies and television portray erotic activity! Prince Charming always instinctively makes just the right moves to have his lover melting in his arms — never needing a guiding word from

her. Romantic as this tale appears, however, its heroine is ultimately a thoroughly passive person with no unique qualities. (Does anyone really believe that all women have the same "buttons"?) The woman who identifies with this heroine must *wait, hope* and *pray* that her erotic needs are met. Consciously or unconsciously, she is endorsing the idea that women are sexual *responders*, with no interest in sex unless aroused by someone else. Needless to say, this deprives a woman of expression and fulfillment of her sexual potential.

"Sex is dirty." If you're like most people, you've probably had urges to say something erotic to your lover or tell her what to do to turn you on better. And, like most, you probably stifled that urge. Our culture has not made it easy to talk or listen rationally, intimately or in a playful way about sex. Instead, the odds are that at home you were exposed primarily to awkwardness, embarrassment, misinformation, or avoidance of honest discussions of sex while growing up.

"Sex was never discussed at home except in a derogatory way. The attitude of my parents affected my present reluctance or embarrassment around LoveTalk in or out of bed." *(Ken, 35)*

"At first I found (LoveTalk) difficult. I had a lot of respect for my girlfriend. I felt she might not think I respected her as much, and I have always been taught that sex was something dirty." *(Gabriel, 32)*

"Sex isn't to be discussed." "It's virtually impossible to talk with my lover about sex out of bed. I feel embarrassed discussing the subject because the way I grew up girls were not supposed to talk about sex until they got married." *(Alysha, 34)* "Discussions about sex in or out of bed are difficult for me. This subject has never been easy for me; I was raised in a very conservative home and my husband of six years was not one for talk." *(Chelsea, 29)*

What Inhibits LoveTalk? Personal Anxieties

Along with these unfortunate myths about sex talk, many people have personal concerns that make them reluctant to talk about sex. Here are a few:

"I feel awkward/embarrassed." "I don't have much experience talking about sex." *(Carlos, 20)* "I worry that my lover thinks I'm naive..." *(Jessica, 29)*

"I'll leave myself vulnerable if I expose my sexual needs and insecurities." "Sometimes I tell partners what I really like, and I feel like I've become vulnerable and allowed someone to get one up on me or be able to hold something over me." *(Tony, 38)* "I am really shy and afraid of negative response toward me sexually." *(Lisanne, 27)*

"I don't want to hurt my lover's feelings." (If I disclose my true feelings, I might make him feel inadequate or offend his sensibilities): "I'd really like to watch some explicit stuff but I know she'd be really upset and flip out." *(Phil, 33)* "I don't talk about sex because I think my lover doesn't want to do the things I would like him to do." *(Bobbi, 42)* "What stops me from talking about sex is being afraid I, as a female, will appear too 'forward' in his eyes." *(Charlene, 35)*

"I don't feel I'm being heard." "I've told him over and over how I want to be touched, to no avail." *(Liesl, 37)*

It's no wonder so many of us feel reluctance about LoveTalk! On the other hand, mustering up the courage to bring informative, frank or playful LoveTalk into your erotic encounters can reap great rewards and make the risks involved well worth it. You'll learn to alter your perspective and challenge the beliefs that block the way to successful LoveTalk in the exercises in this and the next two chapters.

Guidelines for Sex-cessful LoveTalk Sessions

• *Suspend judgment.* Make a commitment to suspend judgement of yourself or your lover. *All* LoveTalk should

begin from a fundamentally non-judgmental perspective
("I'm OK; you're OK"). If you're not feeling good about your
own erotic needs and preferences, you're more likely to
become hypersensitive or challenging when discussing
sensitive erotic matters with your lover.

• *Pick a time in advance.* This is a very individual matter,
so you and your lover need to think about where you're the
most comfortable. Your setting should be free of distractions
such as television, radio, the telephone, or your pager.

• *Don't have a session right after sex.* Don't hold these
discussions immediately after lovemaking, especially if you'll
be making suggestions for improvement. Similarly, don't
decide to have LoveTalk when you know you'll be hungry
or rushed.

• *Pick a relaxed, "vertical" setting.* The possibilities are
endless: a couch, bed, hammock, hillside, or whatever suits
your tastes as lovers. Or you might try, as other lovers have
successfully, to talk in the car! Cars provide comfort and
privacy, and many people feel freer to talk when not making
eye contact.

• *Establish physical contact.* When the setting permits it,
settle in a position that makes you feel especially connected
to your lover. You might rest your head in your lover's lap
(or vice versa). Or you might sit over a fabulous dinner,
looking at each other and touching affectionately. Or you
might prefer to sit or recline side by side.

• *Avoid demeaning labels or comments.* Stay firmly away
from words and phrases — such as "sick," "frigid," "pervert"
— that suggest there is something wrong with your lover.
LoveTalk should never be demeaning or hostile, in or out of
bed. After all, your lover is sharing intimate thoughts and
feelings.

• *Provide feedback on how sessions went.* When you're finished, give each other a little feedback about your LoveTalk session and what you gained from it.

• *Pick a situation that feels comfortable for you.* LoveTalk goes more sex-cessfully when you feel relaxed and secure. Maybe it's on an exotic vacation trip. Or on a not-so-exotic walk, hand-in-hand near home. It could even be over the phone. The secret is to seek a circumstance that creates the greatest comfort and the least concerns.

"Some of the easiest times for discussing sex have come after we have both watched a very passionate scene in a movie together and we talk about what we liked, and what turned us on the most, what we would like to try next, and so on. It's probably when we communicate the best because it's like we're critiquing somebody else, so there is no room for blame or embarrassment to either of us." *(Rayelle, 32)* "The easiest time is talking on the phone and the hardest is face-to-face." *(Emalie, 27)* "We're most comfortable when we're alone somewhere — but not at home, maybe out driving." *(Octavio, 35)* "After having dinner or lying around with my lover watching television is best." *(Abe, 29)* "One-on-one in a quiet setting is the easiest and most comfortable time for us." *(Judy, 32)*

SEX-CESSFUL LOVETALK EXERCISE
''Exploring Each Other's Erotic Vocabulary''

For all the information you've been exposed to on television, in books, and in off-color remarks, the odds are you still don't have an adequate erotic vocabulary to clearly describe your specific sex needs. Most people don't even feel comfortable using the vocabulary they do have. In some instances, the words you use or know are vague or lacking (e.g., "down there"). In others, they may be harsh or rather ridiculous: (e.g., "banging").

The following exercise is designed to let your lover know what specific words are turn-ons and turn-offs to you. It will also increase your own comfort with sexual terms and even present the opportunity to create new and more positive ones that are uniquely shared with your lover. When you've completed the exercise, you will have a new, more positive, and playful LoveTalk vocabulary.

- Plan on fifty minutes to carry out this specific exercise in an uninterrupted setting.
- Use the "sentence stems" below to launch your LoveTalk.
- Decide who will speak first and have that person read the first stem out loud and give her views. Alternate after that.
- When the first person has said what he or she feels, the other should then say how she or he would complete it.
- When it's your turn to speak, be gentle, clear, and specific.
- When it's your turn to listen, be respectful, nonjudgmental, and actively interested.

Sentence stems:

> "If I ever use a sexual word that bothers you, what
>   I'd like you to do is..."
>
> "Sexual words or expressions that are guaranteed to
>   turn me off are..."
>
> "Something sexual I've never really had a good word
>   or expression to describe is..."
>
> "Some new terms I'd really enjoy using/hearing are..."
>
> "The words for my genitals I like the best are..."
>
> "The words for my genitals I like least are..."
>
> "The words for breasts I like best are..."
>
> "The words for breasts I like least are..."
>
> "The words for my nipples I like best are..."
>
> "The words for my nipples I like least are...."
>
> "The words for buttocks I like best are..."
>
> "The words for buttocks I like least are...."
>
> "The words for intercourse I like best are..."
>
> "The words for intercourse I like least are..."
>
> "The words for oral sex I like best are..."
>
> "The words for oral sex I like least are..."
>
> "The words for anal sex I like best are..."
>
> "The words for anal sex I like least are..."

Now that you've learned to feel less constrained about sexual vocabulary, it's time to put LoveTalk to practical use. In the next two chapters, you and your lover will use LoveTalk to open lines of sexual communication and resolve conflicts in ways you never thought possible (Vertical LoveTalk); and then use it to add spice and sizzle to your lovemaking (Horizontal LoveTalk).

2

VERTICAL LOVETALK
"Telling your lover what you like"

"I haven't talked to my lover about what is pleasing to me."

(Laura, 27)

"I'm still thinking about how I can ask her to do oral sex."

(Fred, 32)

"I wish I could tell him that he always does the same thing, and I don't necessarily enjoy his style of lovemaking."   (Kelly, 35)

"I have discussed before that I think he's too passive. I would really love for him to ravish me spontaneously!"   (Marissa, 32)

"I want to tell him how to stimulate me manually. I know exactly what I like; I just don't know how to tell him. He did it right once, and I told him to remember what he did because it felt great, but I'm not sure he knows that other things he does don't do a thing for me."   (Pauline, 46)

Sex doesn't begin under the sheets... it's important to realize that a lot of the attitudes and feelings that occur during love making result from the interactions between you and your lover all evening, all day, all week... When your conversations out of bed get past the events of the day, the latest tax bills, horror stories on the evening news and the trash bag that the dog just tore up... you may begin to have thoughts of love. It's at this point that vertical LoveTalk begins: the "out-of-bed" language you use to express your thoughts and feelings about your sexual relationship with your lover.

Some LoveTalk of course, is appropriate at those times when you're in the heat of passion ("A little to the left..." "Your elbow is in my ribs!") — or in the warm glow immediately after. Other topics are better discussed later, when you are both vertical again ("Next time, let's try..."). Suggesting an activity or making a request that inadvertently upsets your lover could provoke anger or embarrassment if it comes during lovemaking. It's better to save concerns for vertical LoveTalk. You're more likely to express your feelings and preferences in a positive manner — without seeming to attack your lover — if you wait. We'll discuss the "horizontal LoveTalk" in the next chapter. For now, let's concentrate on your out-of-bed conversations about lovemaking.

Sexual preferences. One key to great lovemaking is to communicate clearly and fearlessly out of bed about sexual preferences and desires. Even if you've been together for years, you're likely to discover new things about your lover that can enrich and deepen your sexual connection. This kind of vertical LoveTalk provides a wonderful opportunity to share other kinds of turn-ons, from sexual activities and positions to places you'd like to try having sex. When you avoid positive LoveTalk about new things you want to try, you simply condemn your sex life to the same boring, frustrating old routine.

Constructive problem solving. This is one of the most important forms of vertical LoveTalk. It resolves problems before they get worse. When you avoid sexual concerns and conflicts, you set the stage for a deteriorating sex life that threatens your entire relationship. When you discuss them constructively, you open the way to hotter lovemaking. Common disagreements are about specific activities you do or don't like, the basic quality of your lovemaking, and frequency of sex.

Specific activities you do or don't like. "The issue of positioning during actual intercourse often surfaces as a disagreement... he prefers the traditional missionary position, while I frequently am not aroused in this position. Although we have tried other positions (such as me on top), he continues to maneuver so he is on top..." *(Barbara, 42)*

Basic quality of lovemaking. "I felt that he was centered primarily on his needs and that he viewed sex as one-sided. It was unsettling... I felt more emotionally distant from him... I felt uncertain about our ability to compromise." *(Renee, 29)*

Frequency of sex. "If it were up to me we would make love three times a day. But she's basically content with once a week." *(Carlos, 33)*

Guidelines for Using Positive LoveTalk

If you've experienced explosive, painful and ongoing conflicts about sexual matters, your vertical LoveTalk skills need to be more finely honed. The following guidelines will help you maximize the benefits and minimize the risks of vertical LoveTalk:

• *Pick a comfortable time and way to introduce vertical LoveTalk.* Particularly when broaching a sensitive sexual topic, pick a situation that will put you and your lover at ease.

"I usually bring up the subject by sharing with him a movie I watched or an article I read. At the beginning of my relationship, I wanted to know what my lover thought about oral sex so I shared with him an article in a magazine." *(Vanessa, 32)* "One time we were sitting around watching TV and a talk show came on about male fantasies." *(Steve, 38)* "I just started the conversation by saying that I really liked what we had done the night before..." *(Beth, 34)*

• *Avoid contempt or creating defensiveness.* In vertical LoveTalk, it's important to avoid all the common verbal mannerisms — such as "you" criticisms — that create defensiveness. It can launch both of you into a negative spiral of accusation and counter-accusation. The same is true of statements and tones that suggest contempt. The anger these arouse is one step away from the final stage in communication breakdown: stonewalling. Furthermore, the disintegrating pattern of contempt-defensiveness-stonewalling is a virtual guarantee of future break-up.

• *Avoid "why" questions.* Generally speaking, "why" questions are recipes for LoveTalk disaster. Such questions do not invite dialog or reflect an honest interest in resolving differences. Their underlying purpose, whether the person asking them wants to take responsibility for it or not, is judging, blaming, humiliating or otherwise putting your lover on the defensive. *"Why* do we have to have the lights out when we make love?" *"Why* do you have to stay up so late; you know I'm not interested in sex when you crawl into bed after midnight?" *"Why* does it take you such an eternity to have an orgasm?" *"Why* don't you like to make love in the morning?"

• *Avoid absolute statements and questions that use "always" or "never."* These create a defensive, adversarial atmosphere and invariably represent an exaggeration of the truth — and not the truth itself. They're just another verbal trigger that will make your lover defensive. Marry one of these "absolute negatives" to a basic "why" question and you create a verbal "double whammy." Try it with the examples above — you'll see how much more hurtful each phrase becomes. "*Why* does it *always* take you such an eternity to have an orgasm? It *never* took any of the other women I've been with so long."

• *Avoid "should" statements.* Whether phrased as a positive or a negative, "should" statements express negative judgment. Again, this can only produce defensiveness. "You *should* lose weight. Your belly really turns me off." "You *shouldn't* masturbate. No wonder you don't want to have sex with me."

• *Avoid domineering, hostile, or sarcastic tones of voice.* The well known adage, "It's not what you say, it's how you say it" applies especially to destructive LoveTalk. A hostile, "Maybe I'll just have to go elsewhere for sex"; or a sarcastic "I suppose you think you're a great lover"; or a dominating "I'll decide to see a sex therapist when I'm good and ready," all set the stage for a defensive response.

• *Use open-ended questions:* Open-ended questions typically begin with question words, *who, what, when, where, how.* (Remember to avoid *"why."*) By contrast, closed questions restrict your choices to "yes," "no," or some variation such as "maybe." Closed questions such as the following don't leave room for your lover to express his or her own interests: "Do you like oral sex?" "Do you like it when I touch your breasts?" "Does it feel good when I stroke your penis?" "Does touching your clit cause a climax?"

You're much more likely to learn about pleasing your lover from open-ended phrases like these: "How do you feel about sex?" "How do you especially like to be touched?" "How do you like your penis stroked?" "What's the easiest way for you to climax?"

• *Be specific.* Make your LoveTalk messages specific. Notice how the following clarifies exactly what kind of oral sex you like to receive: "I love soft, gentle kisses on my clitoris and inner lips. That really turns me on." This is a surer guarantee of getting what you want than a vague: "I like it when you go down on me."

• *"Stroke" each other frequently:* The best way to keep your relationship stable and happy is to stroke and validate your lover with positive LoveTalk every day. Set your goal on a minimum ratio of five positive validations ("strokes") for every negative piece of feedback or critical statement you give. That's the formula for growing a successful marriage, according to Dr. John Gottman's pioneering studies at the University of Washington. Maintaining this ratio is even more crucial when you're talking about something as personal and sensitive as sex. Don't keep your positive thoughts to yourself! Spend them lavishly on your lover with the kinds of statements that show you love and value her or him as a sexual being: "I love those pants on you; you look so sexy in them." "You're such a great lover."

Hint: Compliments not directly relating to sex also add a lot to your sex life — especially when it comes to making him or her receptive to lovemaking. A lover who is feeling appreciated or validated in the rest of your life together with strokes — "Thanks for helping me clean up," "I love how nice you are to my family," "You're a great cook" — is a lot more likely to feel like being sexual with you.

• *Steer yourself into positive LoveTalk.* If you know you have a tendency toward negative LoveTalk, try to retrain yourself. Regardless of who triggered it, take some of the responsibility and do your best to steer your LoveTalk back on a constructive track. Make every effort to respond to your lover non-defensively by:

- Focusing only on the constructive portions of LoveTalk
- Using constructive LoveTalk
- Suggesting a "time-out" if needed
- Sticking to one sexual issue you'd like to resolve and not digressing off the subject
- Employing a "how can we...?" problem-solving approach.

There may be times when a flexible "we'll do it your way this time, my way next time" approach is the best solution. Remember that there's a big difference between feeling uncomfortable about something and feeling repelled or that your values are being completely compromised.

VERTICAL LOVETALK EXERCISE I
"Paraphrasing: Learning to Mirror Your Lover's Meaning"

Paraphrasing is a particularly powerful LoveTalk tool. In paraphrasing, you re-state your best understanding of what your lover just said. Your lover might tell you: "Our lovemaking seems like a drag these days; we just seem to do it hit and miss, when we can spare fifteen minutes. I'm not very satisfied with it." Your typical reaction might be to respond more to how this statement made you feel than what your lover actually said. You might see the remarks as critical and blaming and become defensive and counter-blaming yourself: "It's not my fault! You're the one who wanted to move out into the 'burbs where the crime rate is lower and the schools are better. That adds an hour a day to my commute."

Restating what your lover has said prevents what you say from seeming blaming or dismissive. If you were to paraphrase what was said above it might come out something like: "You seem to be saying that we aren't devoting the time and attention to our sex life that we used to, and that you'd like us to start making it a higher priority; is that right?" Notice that whether your paraphrasing is completely accurate or not, you've opened the door to further dialog about the subject in a collaborative, nonjudgmental way.

Paraphrasing shows you are listening attentively and makes your lover feel heard, understood, cared for. A woman is particularly likely to respond positively to her lover when he shows he heard what she said — and negatively when he does not. Paraphrasing helps men prevent LoveTalk from slipping into the typical "advice-giving" male communication style.

Whenever anyone starts dispensing advice, however well intended, she is also automatically putting herself in a "one-up" position. By implication, she has *the* solution or answer to a problem, and the other person doesn't. This might also be called the "Oh Great Wise One" style.

You'll do *far* better in your LoveTalk, man or woman, if you stick to paraphrasing and resist the temptation to give unsolicited advice. If this is a habit of yours, as it is for many, making a genuine effort to break it will reap rich dividends in increased communication, closeness and approval from your lover.

You're not being asked to give up your problem-solving skills here. You're being asked to give up *unsolicited* advice. (Of course, if your lover clearly asks for advice, or you'd like some, say so by all means! There's a *big* difference between solicited and unsolicited advice.)

The exercise below is designed to train you away from defensiveness, blaming and criticism — and into paraphrasing.

1. As always with vertical LoveTalk sessions, pick a time when the two of you can be alone and undisturbed.

2. Decide which of you will go first.

3. The first lover should state a concern or problem about lovemaking.

4. The other lover then tries to rephrase what the first said — without adding anything.

5. If the first lover doesn't feel the meaning was understood, repeat the concern again. And the lover listening should re-paraphrase what she or he thought was meant.

6. When the person expressing concerns is satisfied that she has been understood, it becomes the other lover's turn to express a concern.

7. Throughout the process, pay attention to your *non-verbal* communications: tone of voice, eye contact, facial expression, body posture, gestures. Be sure your body is saying the same thing as your words!

8. Continue this exchange for about half an hour.

9. Afterward, share any thoughts you have about the exercise and its effect on understanding.

10. Use paraphrasing in all your future vertical and horizontal LoveTalk.

VERTICAL LOVETALK EXERCISE II
"Use I-Statements Instead of Criticism"

Everyone's hurt by what they perceive as criticism of their lovemaking. When you do need to tell your lover you want him or her to do something different or stop doing something that doesn't turn you on, it's critical to use a direct style of LoveTalk — what family therapists and other communication specialists call *"I-statements."* Findings from the University of Washington's "marriage lab" show that only this kind of feedback distinguishes a statement from a criticism, or worse, a contemptuous comment.

Only a *statement* serves as a helpful LoveTalk tool. It focuses on a particular action or situation that you wish were otherwise. It opens the way to a constructive dialog with your lover.

Statements make clear you are airing the issue as the first step on the road to resolution. By contrast, *criticism* is global and typically entails blaming or accusing your lover. "You're the one who..." or "It's your fault that..." *Contempt,* which is also a global attack, simply adds insult to the criticism, often by name-calling.

Notice the difference in both the tone and specificity of the following three ways someone might express dissatisfaction with a lover's abrupt departure from the bed to clean up after ejaculation:

(Criticism): "You're so uptight after we have sex."

(Contempt): "You're such a neat-freak; what's the matter with you?"

(Statement): "It's frustrating to me when you get up to wash right after you ejaculate; it breaks the mood of closeness I feel with you then."

The last may not sound like at it at first, but this is definitely an "I-statement" — a direct LoveTalk message. It personalizes the speaker's distress and is not judgmental.

Don't take the suggestion to use "I" LoveTalk messages too literally; in other words, such statements do not inevitably begin with the word "I." Nor does merely prefacing the critical comment with an "I think" automatically make it an "I" LoveTalk message ("I think that you are uptight after we have sex"). It still remains a generalized, global attack and slur on your lover's character that typically evokes nonproductive, defensive responses

The following exercise will start you on the road to replacing any tendency you have toward critical comments and global "you" statements with positive "I" statements. (I have provided sample responses to help get you started. But you should restate each in your own terms, anyway.)

Read the four negative, global "you" complaints below.

Turn each into a specific "I" LoveTalk statement.

1. *"You're so inconsiderate when we have sex."* ("I" LoveTalk alternative): "I frequently give you oral sex but I don't receive it as often as I would like."

2. *"You're in such a rush when we have sex."* ("I" LoveTalk alternative): "I wish you could make it last longer when we have sex."

3. *"You must be a sex addict."* ("I" LoveTalk alternative): "I don't want sex as often as you do."

4. *"You turn me off when we have sex."* ("I" LoveTalk alternative): "I get turned off when you come to bed drunk and sweaty."

VERTICAL LOVETALK EXERCISE III
"Using Door-opening Phrases to Share Sexual Turn-ons and Offs"

Door-opening phrases encourage your lover to elaborate on his or her wants and feelings and keep LoveTalk going. They signal, "Tell me more about what you like/don't like" and, "I'm listening..." When you use door-opening phrases you are likely to learn a lot of interesting things about your lover's sexual preferences you never suspected before.

Below are some door-opening sentence stems that will guide you and your lover through a rewarding Vertical LoveTalk session. These sentence stems provide an opportunity to explore and share your sexual likes and dislikes. You don't have to go through every single stem at one sitting. There is so much to discover about each other sexually you'll want to explore further in other sessions. You may even want to create sentence stems that more closely reflect your own interests, situation or needs.

When you are responding to something your lover says, practice paraphrasing and asking open-ended questions. Avoid comments that imply negative labels or judgments. Remember, your lover is giving the gift of honest disclosure when she or he speaks.

A note of caution: Couples and individuals differ in the amount of disclosure they can handle about sexual matters during any one discussion. This is especially true when it comes to sensitive matters like past sexual histories or abuse. Before beginning this exercise, be sure to agree that you will each inform the other when a topic makes you uncomfortable—and that you'll then go on to another subject. Don't feel obligated to "tell all" if there is something that, in your better judgment, should be deferred until another time (this particularly applies to the stems below with asterisks [*]).

The steps are the same as those for the "Exploring Each Other's Sexual Vocabulary" exercise in the preceding chapter.

1. Pick a time and place where you will be undisturbed for about fifty minutes.

2. Alternate who reads each stem first.

3. The speaker should complete the sentence by expressing his views on the subject.

4. The other person can then read the stem and fill in with her own personal likes or dislikes, or she can react to what her lover has said first (see above for guidelines).

5. The person reading the stem should be gentle, clear and specific.

6. The one listening should be respectful, non-judgmental and actively interested.

Sentence Stems:

"Something I really like about our sexual connection is..."
"What really turns me on is..."
"What moves me to orgasm is..."
"What brings me to the most intense orgasms is..."
"What I like about your orgasm is..."
"Something you could do that really turns me on and would get me really in the mood for sex is..."
"Something sexual I don't really like is..."
"Something I'm curious about is..."
"Something sexual I've always wanted to try is..."
"Something sexual I'd like to try but feel a little awkward or embarrassed about is..."
"Something I saw/read recently about sex that intrigued me and could pertain to us is..."
"One thing I'd like from you sexually is..."
*"One of my sexual secrets is..."
*"The thing I most want to tell you that I haven't yet is..."
*"Something I'm embarrassed to ask you is..."
*"One of my sexual fantasies is..."
*"When I make love I like to..."
*"Something I think would improve our sex life is..."
*"One thing that worries me sexually (or during sex) is..."
*"When we (have sex, make love) I feel ..."

(Add your own stems if there's something you want to address that is not covered above.)

VERTICAL LOVETALK EXERCISE IV
"Staying Calm"

Calm yourself down when something you hear upsets you during vertical LoveTalk. Remaining calm is the key step in resolving sexual differences with vertical LoveTalk. Remaining or getting back to calm is particularly important if you are a man. It takes less negativity to set off the emotional and physical overload called "physiologic flooding" in males. Physiologic overload then triggers defensiveness, combativeness and a strong desire to remove oneself from an upsetting scene.

Once physiologic flooding sets in, your capacity for constructive LoveTalk plummets. Train yourself to stay calm by taking "time outs" when you notice that you are starting to experience physiologic arousal. It's vital both you and your lover recognize the importance of time-outs — and always respond in a positive manner when either of you requests one.

1. During discussions of sexually charged or touchy issues, monitor your mental state for feelings of defensiveness, argumentiveness and the urge to "get away."

2. Check your pulse and call for a time-out whenever it goes up more than 10%.

3. During a time-out, take slow, deep breaths and do whatever else helps you calm down — whether it's a hot shower, listening to soothing music, or a walk around the block. (Alcohol is not recommended here.) See also Love Skills Tips for Anxious Moments, page 199.

4. Replace thoughts that reinforce distress and physiologic arousal, such as "Things will never get better with our sex life," with distress-reducing thoughts such as, "Somehow, we'll figure this out."

5. Don't resume the discussion until at least twenty minutes have passed. (If you're like most people, you'll think you've calmed down before you actually have. It typically takes twenty minutes or so to for your body to return to normal and your pulse rate is the surest gauge.)

The exercises in this chapter may be repeated until the two of you agree through vertical LoveTalk that the sexual lines of communication between you have opened significantly. When you feel that you are ready to go further — and ready to use horizontal LoveTalk to steam up your relationship and heighten your erotic enjoyment — turn to the next chapter.

3

HORIZONTAL LOVETALK
"It keeps everything very focused and very hot"

"I love when he talks to me when we're having sex. I get even more excited knowing he, too, is excited." (Nancy, 33)

"LoveTalk makes me feel wanted and desirable." (Sandra, 26)

"LoveTalk gets me going and I feel my lover is really into it." (Scott, 35)

"LoveTalk is a very important part of stimulation, because all the senses are in use, and it adds to the physical and emotional aspect." (Charles, 42)

"Without LoveTalk, sex would be very boring." (Suzanne, 27)

"LoveTalk puts both people in the right time and place. There's no chance to be thinking about other things — bills, problems, whatever. It keeps everything very focused and very hot." (Bianca, 37)

"LoveTalk makes me feel loved, not used." (Lisa, 29)

"LoveTalk is terrific and makes the experience more exciting." (Alejandro, 36)

There's nothing like horizontal LoveTalk to add sizzle to your sex life! Horizontal LoveTalk during lovemaking adds new dimensions to your sexual pleasure. LoveTalk while you're horizontal heightens arousal by combining verbal and non-verbal eroticism. Sharing your erotic passion for your lover in this way transforms amorous interludes into a "multimedia" event.

Restricting yourself to nonverbal expression of your desire or degree of satisfaction means omitting one of your sexiest "organs" — your voice! Horizontal LoveTalk enhances eroticism by providing each other guidance in how and what to do next, adds to enjoyment with a dash of playfulness, builds intimacy with "sweet nothings," and spices the mix with a few well-chosen "naughty" expressions.

Six types of horizontal LoveTalk can fuel your erotic pleasure:

Sweet Nothings LoveTalk
Instructional LoveTalk
Likes-and-Dislikes LoveTalk
Playful LoveTalk
Naughty LoveTalk
Nonverbal LoveTalk

You're not alone if you feel some inhibitions about using one or more forms of horizontal LoveTalk. It makes lots of folks feel awkward, vulnerable, unromantic, crude, at a loss for words and fearful of rejection.

Sweet Nothings LoveTalk

"Sweet nothings" are expressions of caring and devotion that you and your lover utter during amorous sessions. Sweet nothings LoveTalk ranges from "I love you," to "Your hair smells great." Though called "nothings," they are actually very important "somethings" that deepen intimacy, closeness and the feeling of being loved. These are the expressions that let you know you are desired, valued and appreciated.

Makes you feel sexy: "I like sweet nothings the best because they are normally about how great I am, which is an ego booster." *(Mike, 32)* "The LoveTalk I adore most is when he looks into my eyes and tells me how beautiful I am — because I don't regard myself as a beautiful person." *(Marla, 42)* "I like it when he tells me he loves me or that he finds me sexy because I feel both special and attractive." *(Sheila, 35)*

Builds intimacy: "Sweet nothings make me feel closer to him and very loved." *(Christine, 39)* "I prefer my lover to whisper sweet nothings in my ears. I literally melt when he says beautiful words of love." *(Keisha, 28)*

For some people, saying sweet nothings is difficult. They become tongue-tied, feel vulnerable, or wonder if they sound sincere.

Clams you up: "Not knowing what to say keeps me from saying sweet nothings." *(Don, 32)*

Creates feelings of vulnerability: "I find it very hard to say sweet nothings. The combination of lovemaking and expressing my innermost emotions at the same time is allowing myself to become too vulnerable." *(Rafi, 36)*

Evokes concerns about sincerity: "I feel like I'm getting too mushy." *(Kim, 33)*

Learning what specific sweet nothings your lover would like to hear will reduce any concern about knowing what to say. You can also agree to only use expressions you're comfortable with or that don't feel phony to you.

Instructional LoveTalk

"Instructional LoveTalk" refers to the requests lovers make to keep on or to change the way they are making love. The only way you can each get just exactly what arouses you most during erotic encounters is to share *what* you want and *when* you want it. No matter how well you know each other's sexual preferences, your lover can't possibly know what would arouse you most at *that* moment in *that* lovemaking session.

Actively telling your lover what you want her or him to do — or to stop doing — has many benefits. Instructional LoveTalk:

Helps avoid a routine pattern based on assumptions that you "always" want the same things

Can stop an activity you're not enjoying

Provides an opportunity to suggest new activities you've never tried before

Ends the frustrating passive "wait-hope-pray" approach to getting what you want

Allows you to relax and remain fully focused on experiencing pleasure without wondering if you're pleasing your lover.

Lets you know you are satisfying your lover: "I like to know what she really wants, and how I'm there to please her. I always ask her to tell me what she likes and how she wants it." *(Jack, 38)* "It gives me the feedback that I desire and leads me in the right direction. Being positively encouraged can be such a turn-on." *(Samantha, 45)*

Enhances lovemaking: "It takes the pressure off both of us so we're not so worried about performing." *(Connie, 33)* "I would prefer it if she talked more. I like to know when I am doing something right or wrong or if it feels good or bad." *(Matt, 37)*

However, much as we would like to guide our lovers during lovemaking, we often fear putting our wants into words. Embarrassment, guilt, and concern about hurting your lover's feelings are usually the culprits. Speaking up:

Minimizes embarrassment: "Sometimes specific instructions are embarrassing." *(Erica, 32)* "Sometimes I feel embarrassed when asking my lover for oral sex even though I know she likes to do it." *(Derek, 31)*

Reduces concern over hurt feelings: "I'm very inhibited because my lover gets very defensive when I tell him to touch me here or there... but it also hurts me because I want to grow with him sexually." *(Tammy, 29)* "I feel like I'm being too bossy and commanding." *(Lynnette, 35)*

The secret to positive instructional LoveTalk is to be sure what you say comes across as *requests, not commands.* Make your guidance sultry, flirtatious, playful or gentle.

If you experience anxiety or embarrassment at being guided, let your lover know how you'd like comments phrased or delivered. And let go of the mistaken notion that you should be able to divine what your lover wants by mental-telepathy ("If you *really* loved me, you'd know..."), or that the request is a criticism.

Likes-and-Dislikes LoveTalk

The comments that give you and your lover feedback about what is and isn't turning you on during sex are "Likes-and-Dislikes LoveTalk." These are usually simple, straightforward requests to continue or change a particular activity. Likes-and-Dislikes LoveTalk lets you and your lover know if you are pleasing one another.

Likes-and-Dislikes LoveTalk can provide encouragement to keep on going when everything is going right: "That's great; you're driving me wild!" "I love it when you nibble my earlobes like that." It can also provide crucial negative feedback when lovemaking misfires amorously: "I don't like the way that feels." "That doesn't turn me on as much as..."

Most of us enjoy hearing the "likes" parts of Likes-and-Dislikes LoveTalk. We like to know we are pleasing our lovers. However, we are sometimes reluctant to verbalize the fact that our lovers are pleasing us for fear they will consider us shameless.

Why we like to hear "likes" LoveTalk: "I like knowing that what I do makes him feel good. Like when he says my naked body feels so good next to his." *(Hannah, 36)* "The best turn-on for me is when a woman is having an orgasm and tells me." *(Greg, 40)* "I love affirmative talk such as 'Oh yes, you feel so good' or 'I feel so good inside you.' " *(Christine, 39)*

But most people have a very difficult time dealing with negative feedback — whether giving it or hearing it. Phrasing and delivery play an important part in determining how you or your lover react to negative feedback. So do your individual sensitivities.

Why we are afraid to express "dislikes" LoveTalk: "Asking my lover to stop what she is doing or to do something different is the hardest. It might hurt her feelings." *(Allen, 29)* "I don't use 'dislike' talk because it takes away from the romance." *(Jan, 42)*

When you're on the receiving end and it's phrased and delivered gently, don't take it as a personal attack or a put-down of your lovemaking. When you are the one making the comment, don't say anything that could be taken as derogatory or demeaning. You'll get a lot more mileage from a gentle, "I'd like to do something else now" than a harsh, "I have to stop; you're taking too long."

Playful LoveTalk

"Playful LoveTalk" is just that — playful! It's a way of talking to your lover about and during sex that's fun, exciting and very personal. It includes teasing, laughing, using special words and phrases that the two of you coined and share. Playful LoveTalk is spontaneous, "now"-focused and the most creative form of horizontal LoveTalk. Playful

LoveTalk can transform dull encounters into sexy turn-ons, because it:

Increases closeness: "My favorite kind of LoveTalk is playful — that involves a little teasing because it makes me feel that we are closer, that is, friends, as well as lovers." *(Chitra, 38)*

Develops a private vocabulary: "Playful LoveTalk comes very easy because we have created our own silly language that only we can appreciate and relate to. We made up names for parts of our body and sexual positions/activities we engage in..." *(Tom, 28)*

Enhances erotic creativity: "Fantasy, playful LoveTalk is the greatest turn-on for me. I have a lover who is an actor and during lovemaking we will often become someone else, and the other one follows the lead... these are personalities or occupations. For example, I say 'I feel like your whore' and he takes it from there." *(Rhonda, 45)*

Makes sex fun: "We have one hell of a good time playing together." *(Howard, 41)* "Playful is the most enjoyable LoveTalk for me; if it's not fun, why bother?" *(Connor, 27)*

As with the other forms of LoveTalk, if being erotically playful with words seems awkward or difficult initially, give yourself a little time — and you'll discover just how much fun has been missing from your lovelife.

Naughty LoveTalk

"Naughty LoveTalk" involves the use of the very "forbidden" slang terms most of us have been taught to think of as "dirty" and "graphic." But at amorous moments, terms that might ordinarily be considered naughty express uninhibited arousal and desire. Precisely *because* they are forbidden, hearing and saying them can have a profoundly erotic effect and stoke intense passion.

Because naughty LoveTalk is explicitly erotic, you may feel awkward about using it or letting your lover use it. If these words make you uncomfortable, remember that they are being used not to demean or shock but to express how deeply you and your lover turn each other on. And if saying them yourself brings your lover to new levels of arousal, aren't you fortunate to be able to bestow so wonderful a gift?

Most people feel some inhibitions about engaging in naughty LoveTalk at first. Embarrassment and being looked down on by their lover are prime concerns.

(While I strongly suggest you try naughty LoveTalk, I realize that some readers, due to their personal values will not wish to participate. Although I do not believe that the use of such words is harmful, I can certainly respect your decision to refrain. But from my clients' experience I know that there are many benefits — and little harm — for those who are able to shed their inhibitions and give it a try.)

Fear of how you will sound: "Either I feel like a whore when I talk dirty or I think I sound ridiculous." *(Laura, 42)*

Fear you'll turn your lover off: "Sometimes I feel just plain embarrassed to use taboo words. Also, I'm afraid (the words) won't be reciprocated." *(Marvin, 52)* "I am wondering whether or not he will like hearing graphic language." *(Patty, 47)* "I like it myself, but my current lover is rather shy about using graphic words and I find myself becoming rather timid about using them." *(Antonio, 28)*

Fear of being judged negatively: "I am inhibited... for fear of being judged as sex-crazed or perverted. I fear my lover's reaction and don't allow myself to be naughty in certain ways." *(Amy, 35)*

Those who let fear keep naughty LoveTalk out of their lives miss one of nature's most powerful aphrodisiacs. Many couples who embellish lovemaking with graphic words and forbidden phrases find it stokes the fires of passion.

Fuels arousal: "Graphic LoveTalk is very sexy and makes me hot." *(Todd, 37)* "Dirty talk makes my erotic experience ten times better." *(Theresa, 29)* "Naughty LoveTalk is a turn-on for me. It provides the richest atmosphere for fantasy." *(Michael, 30)* "It's the greatest kind of LoveTalk. It is so free and lets the barriers down that it becomes such a turn-on." *(Anne, 53)* "The thing that turns her on the most is when I describe what I'm doing to her or going to do to her in a erotic way. 'I'm going to wash you, then shave you, then lick you.' " *(Josh, 26)*

Though you may experience embarrassment or shame at first, the more you use naughty LoveTalk, the less inhibited you will be. Breaking through the barriers simply takes practice and an open attitude.

Nonverbal LoveTalk

"Sounds" also go with great lovemaking! Moans, groans, sighs, and even breathing all add a richer dimension to lovemaking. Their presence fuels arousal and serves as reassurance that "all is well."

Moaning: "What really drives me crazy is when he starts to breathe very hard and when he begins to moan. That's when I've done a very good job at getting him off." *(Tonya, 40)* "When he groans and moans, which he seldom does, that arouses me." *(Sharon, 37)*

Making noises: "The best is when she is moaning and making noises and begging me to bring her to orgasm." *(Ted, 19)*

Screams: "The greatest turn-on is when my girlfriend screams (but not too loud)." *(Guillermo, 34)*

Breathing: "Something about the way he breathes when he's lying on top on me. The sound is so sweet in my ears." *(Kayla, 22)*

HORIZONTAL LOVETALK EXERCISE I
"Discovering Your Horizontal LoveTalk Preferences"

The first step in adding the spice of horizontal LoveTalk to your erotic encounters is determining what each of you would most and least like to hear or use. Since this involves words and phrases that might cause you discomfort, it's best for you to fill out the quiz below separately. After you've done this on your own, you will share — and begin to practice — your list of preferences together in the next exercise.

    1. Separately, take a look at each of the lists below.

    2. Add your own personal choices to each category.

    3. Place an asterisk by those you like best and draw a line through those that you dislike.

    What sweet nothings would you like to hear? *"I love you so much, sweetheart." "You have the most beautiful eyes I've ever seen." "I feel so close to you." "You have the most gorgeous body." "I love your strong arms."* _____

_____

_____

_____

    What instructional requests would you like to make of your lover? *"Tease my lovebud." "I'd love it if you'd 'go down' on me now." "Can I get on top?" "Give it to me hard now." "Grab my butt."* _____

_____

_____

_____

What "likes" would you like to express during horizontal LoveTalk? *"Nobody does it like you, babe." "You feel so good." "Oh, such sweet torture." "I love being deep inside you." "Your tits are so hard and sexy." "I love it when you go slowly like that."* _____

_____

_____

Which "dislikes" would you like to share? *"That's uncomfortable." "Just a little slower now, darling." "I need a little rest."*_____

_____

_____

What playful things would you like say? *"You horny little devil." "It's time to take a Peter meter reading." "John Henry wants to play in the house now."* _____

_____

_____

_____

What naughty suggestive things have you longed to say — or hear? *"I've been thinking about your sweet lips all day." "I love sucking you." "You know what I'm going to do to you? I'm going to spread your legs and then slowly..." "I love your lustiness." "I love to lick your..."* _____

_____

_____

_____

HORIZONTAL LOVETALK EXERCISE II
"Sharing Your Horizontal LoveTalk Preferences"

This couple exercise will add verbal steam to your erotic encounters in two ways. You and your lover share the words and phrases that turn you on or off the most during love-making. You also determine which expression, or expressions, you'd be aroused using yourself.

If your lover has not used much LoveTalk in the past, you're in for a treat, especially if you've been honest about what you'd most enjoy hearing. Be sure to compliment her or him for these efforts, especially for having the courage to say things she or he may never have said before.

1. Share with each other the list of phrases you find fuel or dampen ardor that you compiled in the preceding exercise.

2. Spend forty-five minutes or more discussing personal turn-ons and turn-offs.

3. Decide which you are and are not willing to experiment with hearing and saying— and make that clear to each other.

4. Add those you are willing to try to your next amorous encounter.

5. If saying any of them out loud makes you feel embarrassed or uncomfortable, practice by yourself for a while — perhaps while driving a car or working out. Repeating them like this will help diffuse any inhibitions or awkwardness you may have.

6. Don't be mechanical. Let the words flow naturally from what you're feeling or experiencing at the time. In this way, uttering what your lover would like to hear can become as big a turn-on for you as it is for him or her.

7. Listen to, and enjoy, your lover's LoveTalk, as well!

LoveTalk, in all its forms, is the most basic of Love Skills. Unless you can communicate honestly about what you do and don't like and do and don't need, and unless you can be verbally playful and creative, you can't work together to acquire the skills of BodyLove, LoveTouch and LovePlay that will help you to sustain and intensify an exciting erotic relationship. The words should be honestly your own, but you'll find it helpful to shed your inhibitions and talk openly about your preferences, your body parts, and the sexual activities you and your partner engage in.

In the next chapter, you and your lover will apply LoveTalk to exploring your feelings about your bodies and your sexuality.

Love Skill Two:
BodyLove

4

SEX-CESSFUL BODYLOVE
"When I feel good about my body, I really like making love..."

"I love my body. It can do all sorts of wonderful things and brings me all kinds of delightful sensations. I don't mean just sex — but that too. I love sharing it with my husband and we have great sex together."
(Eva, 38)

"I was raised in a family that was pretty positive about sex and physical displays of affection. My parents hugged and kissed and touched a lot. I've never felt the kind of shame and guilt over enjoying my body during sex that some of my other friends have described."
(Diane, 32)

"I work out a lot. When I feel good about my body, I really like making love with my girlfriend. I know I look good to her and that's a real turn on to me."
(Mark, 34)

"Self-consciousness about my penis size makes me a little gun shy about oral sex."
(Doug, 25)

"My feelings about my breast size affect my willingness to let my lover touch them. I don't mind having sex as long as he doesn't pay a lot of attention to my chest. I tend to shy away if he does. This causes problems because he says he likes my breasts."
(Tschandra, 31)

Now that you know how to add fun and sizzle to your relationship with LoveTalk, it's time to turn the heat up even further and unleash the full emotional and erotic potential of your body with BodyLove. As the above quotes show, how you feel about your body plays a major role in determining the quality of your sex life. It controls how willing you feel to share yourself physically with your lover and how much you enjoy your sexual experiences.

When it comes to keeping life — and the fun — in your lovelife over the long haul, learning the fine art of BodyLove is a must. When you harbor negative feelings about your body — guilt and shame, unhappiness over appearance — it blocks the enthusiasm and pleasure you bring to lovemaking. The less you love your body, the less you are likely to want to share it with your lover. You're both robbed of the passion and fulfillment that are your sexual birthright.

There are many reasons we fail to love — and may actually reject — our bodies, their sexuality, and even the physical aspects of love itself:

Discomfort, embarrassment, shame, or guilt over basic sexual functions.

Self-consciousness about your body's physical responses to sex.

A sense of alienation from your body and lack of interest in its capacity to bring you erotic pleasure.

A lack of trust in your body, ranging from a belief that you'll go "out of control" if you allow yourself to experience orgasm — to the belief that you'll be physically harmed by too much sexual activity.

Fear of being physically rejected by your lover because your body is not "good enough" and you don't deserve sexual love.

A lack of compassion for your own bodily limitations caused by illness, aging, weight gain, etc.

The remainder of this chapter will lead you through a series of steps to a more positive feeling about your body — and your lover's. In the following chapter you will learn to work through any feelings of shame or guilt about the bodily aspects of sex that might be blocking the pathway to a completely rewarding lovelife. The final two BodyLove chapters will help you break free of concerns about body appearance and sex appeal that might be inhibiting sexual expression and enjoyment.

Your Body — And Lovin' It!

Before you can have a great love life — or even a good one — you've got to free yourself from negative attitudes or perceptions you might have about your body. BodyLove, feeling "high" on your body, banishes self-consciousness, frees you from inhibitions and renews your appetite for healthy, passionate lovemaking.

Loving your body enables you to express your sexuality fully, and to rejoice in its powers to bring you profound pleasure, both alone and with your lover. Sharing your body sexually with your lover becomes a natural, inevitable extension of your confidence, pride, intimate knowledge and respect for it.

In fact, loving your body can boost your sexuality in a multitude of ways:

You get turned on by it. You take delight in the sensual pleasures it offers you through *all* of the senses — tastes and smells as well as touch, sight and sound, and you willingly savor them all to heighten your sexual experiences.

You anticipate rewards from it. You expect to enjoy pleasurable experiences and have fulfilling erotic encounters — whether it's a flirtatious wink or earnest anticipation of the next amorous episode.

You have fun with it. You are in touch with its sexually playful and creative possibilities. You enjoy dressing provocatively sometimes and like to have fun with it in and out of bed.

You trust it. You're confident that it will perform well and you make love without worry or concern.

You respect your body. You acknowledge its inner wisdom by paying attention to cues it gives you — whether an eye twitch signals your need to relax, or vaginal lubrication or a growing erection shows your readiness for sexual activity.

You are proud of your body. You have a healthy sense of esteem for it. You feel attractive and sexy — to yourself and to others.

You appreciate its appearance. You know and appreciate its best features, and are happy to be "seen" by your lover with the lights on!

You know your sexual anatomy. You're interested in examining and exploring all of your sexual anatomy — including your genitals. You know which areas are the most sensitive and can find the clitoris, urethral and vaginal opening (if you're a woman), or the frenulum and perineum (if you're a man).

You are comfortable with sexual functions. You are familiar with and aware of your own sexual responses — whether nipple erections, the secretions produced when you are aroused, or the sounds that you make during orgasm.

You take care of it. You maintain it in good condition, knowing it's the basis for increased sexual pleasure.

Exercise, BodyLove and Sex

The first step in coming to love your body is to boost your own perception of the way it looks and performs. Exercise is the one constructive step guaranteed to improve anyone's view of his or her body and desirability. People report that when they are in good physical shape, they make love with greater confidence, comfort and enthusiasm. My own surveys show lovers find exercise enhances their erotic interludes in numerous crucial ways:

Exercise helps you love your body. Studies consistently find that when people exercise, they feel better about their bodies for several reasons. For some, it is due to weight loss or improved appearance from the redistribution of weight and the improvement of muscle tone. For others, it's the increased sense of strength, agility and all around physical competence. "Exercise has had two main positive effects on my sexuality: First, I have more energy and endurance for sex, and second, I feel better about my appearance." *(Kareem, 38)*

Exercise enhances your self-confidence and sexual confidence. Studies show exercise is beneficial to your mental well-being, and has a profound positive effect on depression and anxiety. Self-esteem also rises along with regular exercise. So does the perception of having a sexy body and the willingness to share it with your lover. As some have put it: "Any kind of exercise can make me feel sexy just because exercising makes me feel good about myself. To me, self-confidence is very sexy in other people, so when I feel confident, I feel sexy, too." *(Jeanette, 39)*

Exercise provides you with more energy, including sexual energy. In the long-term, exercise significantly lowers your cholesterol levels, improves your cardiovascular function and boosts hormone levels — resulting in an overall increase in physical functioning and energy level.

Exercise increases your physical capacity to engage in and enjoy sex. Exercise develops endurance, flexibility and strength, which contribute to longer-lasting, more passionate and satisfying lovemaking. Here are typical comments: "Being flexible allows your body to move more into various positions and hold those positions for a longer time without cramping or aching." *(Felicia, 35)* "Exercise has noticeably affected my sexual activity. There were times in the past when I avoided sexual intercourse with my wife because I knew it was going to be so much work; but I've worked out a bit more regularly lately and feel physically up for the challenge now." *(Peter, 40)* "When my lover exercises regularly his stamina during sex increases, as does his sex drive." *(Stephanie, 27)*

Shared Nudity: Getting Comfortable with Your Body

Feeling good about your body is just the beginning of BodyLove. Being comfortable with your body and your lover's body is a necessity. If you're not, you cannot joyously fulfill and embrace your own sexuality — or your lover's. Many couples are able to do exactly that by practicing nudity around each other. Though it might not have occurred to you, quite a number of studies show that lovers who practice nudity have better body images than those who avoid it. When you're not accustomed to seeing each other nude, you're more inclined to measure yourself against some idealized, fantasy image and to say "no" to sex; you are convinced your flaws make you unattractive to others — especially your lover. Going nude around each other typically leads to increased respect for and acceptance of the human form — including your own.

Couples on nudity: "My boyfriend and I recently began sleeping and walking around in the nude. Since this started several months ago, I feel proud of my body." *(Patricia, 32)* "I feel better about my body since we started practicing nudity than I did when I was younger, even though I probably looked better when I was younger." *(Will, 38)* "Nudity enhances my sex life. It introduces a more playful aspect to our relationship." *(Meredith, 29)* "I love being naked.

I don't feel constricted. I love being able to walk across the living room after getting out of the shower." *(Joachim, 26)*

Here are some suggestions for shared activities that other couples reported were beneficial, enjoyable and brought them closer:

- Sleeping nude
- Walking nude from the bathroom after bathing to another room in the house
- Doing household chores, cooking, or working at home nude
- Watching television nude
- "Undressing" for dinner or other meals with your lover
- Skinny dipping
- Dancing nude with your lover
- Showering or bathing with your lover
- Sunbathing in the nude.

Guidelines for Boosting Your Love Life Through Exercise

If you don't exercise, the guidelines below will help get you started. Once you start, they'll help keep you going and — even if you have been exercising for years — show you how to maximize the erotic benefits of a regular routine.

• *Make the time.* If you don't exercise regularly, you probably plead "lack of time." The solution? *Prioritize your time.* When you "can't" make the time to exercise, you're really saying you give a low priority to your health and your sex life.

• *Select an activity you like.* Pick an exercise, or mix of exercises, that you like and that suits you. When you pick something you like, you're much more likely to stick with it. Only you know what appeals to you most — based on your temperament, financial situation, and lifestyle. Jogging is cheap; skiing is expensive. Some people thrive on competitive exercise, such as tennis. Others prefer the tranquil spirituality of cross-country hiking. Still others love the high-energy atmosphere of an aerobics class. If you love to dance, that counts too, as long as you do it *regularly.*

• *Exercise at home if you need to:* If time is a primary concern, or inclement weather sets in for months, by all means exercise at home. Videotaped routines and specialized equipment make home exercise practical and effective.

• *Exercise with others:* Many people find it's easier to exercise consistently if they have a friend who exercises with them. (Of course, it's perfectly all right to exercise alone if that's what you prefer!)

• *Take walks:* Regular walking produces well-documented benefits to your cardiovascular system, overall physical health and sex life.

• *Exercise in moderation.* Studies reveal you don't have to engage in extreme amounts of exercise to reap important physical benefits. In fact, the battle cry to "go for the burn" — also known as "no pain, no gain" — happens to be bad advice. There's no need to exercise to the point of exhaustion or until your muscles are sore. It's not in the best interests of your sex life. At excessive levels, exercise can even impair sexual activity with your lover.

• *Focus on the process, not on goals.* Notice the parallel here between the best way to approach exercise and the best way to approach sex. The more you can focus on the present during "non-sexual" physical activity, the more readily you'll be able to do so during erotic encounters. Abandon goal orientation during sex and savor the moment-to-moment sensations; this a sure way of heightening sensual pleasure. The more you can approach exercise — or *any* physical activity — with this mind set, the more skilled you'll become at savoring *all* sensations, sexual or nonsexual.

• *Exercise with your lover.* Some forms of exercise, such as skiing, tennis, or scuba-diving enhance your sense of sharing common interests. They also give you a chance to be together and interact positively, often in a beautiful environment. Even shared walks offer much more than the physical benefits. They're an excellent opportunity for connecting without distracting interruptions. You reap benefits both to the relationship and physically.

• *Focus on aerobic or aerobic and anaerobic exercise.* Current research shows that aerobic exercise contributes the most to your overall physical health and well-being. On the other hand, both aerobic and anaerobic ("pumping iron") exercise contribute to your appearance, which is pertinent to the quality of your lovemaking.

• *Be flexible.* You'll make the most of any physical exercise regime if you are prepared to adapt rather than abandon it when something disrupts your routine. If your arm is broken and you can't jog as you usually do, switch to power walking. Or try swimming if you have a foot injury and are instructed to avoid putting weight on it. If a change in your work schedule prevents you from going to a health club as often, use an exercise video at home between visits.

• *Pay attention to your body as you exercise.* Exercise can also enhance your sexuality by helping you to develop greater bodily awareness. Focus on the process while exercising: ask yourself things like, "How does my body feel right now?" or "What sensations am I aware of?" Your aim is to become more in tune with your body, to feel more "at home" with it, to appreciate its power, its grace, its sensuality and to treat it with respect.

• *Take advantage of the sexual "second wind" effect.* Many couples have reported enjoying a "sexual second wind" of interest and responsiveness by engaging in sexual activity following exercise! Women in my national survey reported increased desire and arousal. Some even experienced more intense orgasms.

Try making love after a good jog together, for instance. For the best results, take advantage of this second wind within the first hour or two after exercising. The physiological and psychological changes that account for the boost — increased brain activity in the left hemisphere plus an increase of endorphins (both associated with "feeling good" states) — last about that long.

Here's what some people have to say about the sexual second wind: "I am much clearer and more in tune with my body after exercising. It seems that I am able to reach a more intense orgasm more quickly." *(Chantal, 33)* "I feel sexy after working out. My muscles are pumped and I think my body looks better." *(Gabe, 29)* "After exercising, my blood is pumping fast and my adrenaline is flowing. It makes me feel sexy and I usually want to have sex afterward, unless I've overstrained myself." *(Sue, 27)*

SEX-CESSFUL BODYLOVE EXERCISE I
"Exploring Nudity"

Once you begin to feel good about your body through exercise, you are ready for the next step in becoming comfortable with the way your body looks — learning to be comfortable with nudity. Over a period of weeks or a few months, you will discover yourself becoming more at ease with your body and less self-conscious about sharing it with your lover. Odds are that you will spontaneously begin to carry out a variety of activities in the nude. The goal is not being nude all the time at home; instead, it's to enjoy the sense of freedom and naturalness it creates — when the circumstances are appropriate.

1. Each of you list ten activities involving nudity you'd like to try together.

2. Rank them in the order you're most comfortable trying.

3. After you've made your list, start with the item that seems easiest and do it together.

4. As you carry out this activity, reflect from time to time on how your body feels to you and how it is working for you (notice the dexterity of your fingers as you work nude around the house, for instance).

5. At the end of each week, record how you felt about carrying out activities in the nude. Note any changes which occurred in how you perceive or feel about your body.

6. Begin the next week by adding a new activity.

7. Continue this approach until you've tried all the activities on your list.

8. Then try any new ones that have occurred to you — and keep some nudity in your relationship all of the time.

Don't minimize the importance of the BodyLove work you've begun in this chapter. And do keep it up as you proceed through your Love Skills program. You'll reap great rewards from a healthy love for your own body!

The chapter that follows will help you free yourself from any feelings of shame or guilt that you still experience over the sexual aspects of your body. The two chapters after that will help you learn to see yourself as someone who is both attractive and sexy to your lover.

5

SHAMELESS BODYLOVE
"I'll never do that to my own kids"

"I grew up being told my genitals were 'dirty,' and not to touch them. The only time I touch my vagina is in the shower when I'm cleaning my body." (Emma, 47)

"I was around ten years old and was watching TV on the sofa by myself, masturbating. My mother walked in and yelled at me and shamed me. I felt awful. Sometimes later, I would touch myself, but I would feel so guilty, so sinful and so dirty, I would stop. I'll never do that to my own kids." (Kaye, 46)

"I felt most guilty about the untimely erections I would develop when my childhood best friend, who was a girl, would hug me." (David, 37)

You can't learn to love your body or your lover's body until you deal with the deep-seated shame and guilt over the sexual aspects of our bodies that most of us most of us grow up with in this society. Although negative feelings about appearance and sex appeal prevent most of us from giving or getting all we could during lovemaking, shame and guilt can cut us off almost completely from BodyLove's pleasures and possibilities. Unchallenged, they can create disastrous consequences for your erotic relationship.

Feelings of guilt and shame about your body means:

You are less likely to know what turns you on the most and what brings you the greatest sexual fulfillment.

You are less likely to be knowledgeable about your body and your sexual anatomy and function.

You are less likely to share with your lover what knowledge you *do* have of your body's sexual responses and reactions.

You are less likely to fully enjoy the physical pleasures of sex or to make love with your whole body and soul.

You are less likely to pay attention to your sexual anatomy and genitals, or to notice changes that signal something medically amiss, or to report such changes to a physician.

The Anatomy of Shame

Most of us were made to feel guilty about our body's sexual anatomy and our interest in it at a very young age — likely the very first time we were scolded for "touching ourselves," or caught "playing doctor." The idea that exploring the body's potential for sexual pleasure was something "sinful" and "morally wrong" was driven deep into our childish minds. We learned the sexual aspects of our bodies were "dirty" and "ugly" as we learned derogatory slang terms for sexual anatomy and functions — and as we heard cruel adolescent taunts and jokes about the developing sexual characteristics of our schoolmates.

Surveys of practicing marital counselors show that many adults in relationships admit to deep-rooted feelings of sexual shame and guilt that cause them to "freeze up" or physically hold back during lovemaking — robbing lovers of the passion and fire they, and the relationship, deserve. There are lots of reasons for these inhibitions:

"Playing doctor": "I got caught playing 'doctor' twice, once at five with a neighborhood boy and once at nine with a neighbor girl. I really was unsure why it was 'not right,' and not just an okay part of natural curiosity. My mother was very good about explaining that it was natural. But the other kids' parents made a big deal and restricted us from playing together for awhile." *(Rae, 45)*

"Touching yourself": "When my interest in girls picked up, I began masturbating. Society's view on this was (and still is) so negative toward it that I felt very guilty about doing it. It was not until I got into my late teens that I realized that it was an okay thing to do." *(Tim, 36)*

The truth is that touching yourself and playing doctor are perfectly natural, normal activities. Everyone engages in some form of these while growing up. Psychologists call them "juvenile sexual rehearsal play" and say they form a healthy part of exploring and enjoying ourselves as sexual beings. In fact, studies show juvenile sexual rehearsal play is a prerequisite to developing into a sexually confident adult who is able to engage in uninhibited sex play with a lover.

Demeaning sexual vocabulary. Many of the seeds of the sense of shame over the sexual parts of one's body were sown in adolescence. Referred to only in an "underground" slang, our social legacy stigmatizes our sexual anatomy and functions, labeling them as forbidden, illicit and obscene.

Cruel remarks about your body or anatomy: "I was very thin; kids used to tease me and say mean things to me, like 'toothpicks for legs' or 'skinny ninny'." *(Angie, 27)*

"Remember 'Fat Albert,' the Bill Cosby character? That's what my schoolmates used to call me. It really hurt, and I learned to hate my body." *(Frank, 36)*

Self-Pleasuring and Sexual Guilt

Masturbation is one of the greatest pleasures the human body has to offer. Yet for many this form of BodyLove is also the sexual activity that produces the most intense feelings of guilt and shame. Because of misinterpretations of the Bible and ridiculous beliefs about masturbation, you are likely to have grown up believing self-pleasuring is "wrong," a "sin," or "harmful." (The term "masturbation" has such a negative connotation that sexologists use "self-stimulation," "autoeroticism" or "self-pleasuring" instead.)

Some people feel guilty over self-pleasuring because they unnecessarily feel disloyal to their lovers: "Once I masturbated very intensely. I touched myself all over; I licked my fingers and tried to wet myself everywhere. I felt a little like I'd betrayed my husband, and I felt really guilty afterwards." *(Barbie, 38)*

In most cases, self-pleasuring doesn't take anything away from your lover. On the contrary, exploring your own sexuality alone and in private — with the pressure off, so to speak — allows you to discover physical likes, dislikes, turn-ons and the acts that trigger the greatest fulfillment. And these, in turn, you can communicate to your lover.

Studies show that women and men who engage in occasional self-pleasuring make love more frequently, are given higher ratings by their lovers, and enjoy their erotic interludes more than those who don't. This is especially true for women. Decades of scientific surveys show women are more likely to be orgasmic during intercourse when they've had experience stimulating themselves.

SHAME-CHALLENGING BODYLOVE EXERCISE I
"Replacing Messages of Shame and Guilt"

This powerful exercise will help you begin moving beyond guilt and shame by identifying and challenging negative messages you have received about sexuality and your body — no matter the source.

Use this after any situation in which you have felt shame over your body or guilt about an activity.

1. Write the heading "Source" and then identify the source of the message, if you can recall it.

2. Next write the heading "Situation" and describe the circumstances and content of the negative message you received from that source.

3. Finally write the heading "Challenge" and actively challenge it with a more reasonable and rational interpretation of the beliefs, thoughts or activities you have or do now, or used to have or do.

4. Review your list regularly and the challenges will really sink in. (Begin by looking them over several times a week, then weekly, then monthly.)

5. If you find that as you review your list, you come up with additional challenges, add them to your "Challenges" column. Here are a couple of examples:

Source: *Mother*

Situation: *Caught playing doctor*

Challenge: *Most children play doctor. I was five and punished. I was a normal, healthy child with normal curiosity about my body.*

Source: *Unsure*

Situation: *Uncomfortable when my lover wants the lights on and looks intently at my genitals* — and tells me how beautiful they are and what a turn-on they are. I feel self-conscious and ashamed.

Challenge: *My genitals are healthy, formed just as nature intended, and obviously attractive to my lover.*

SHAME-CHALLENGING BODYLOVE EXERCISE II
``Making Friends with Your Genitals — for Women''

Another way to get beyond shame and guilt over your sexual anatomy and functions is to become thoroughly familiar with *all* of your body. This is especially true for those parts you may not know as well, such as your genitals. Studies show that women in particular are likely to harbor negative feelings about the sexual aspects of their bodies. The following exercise, adapted from Betty Dodson's insightful book on self-stimulation, *Sex for One*, will help you move beyond those feelings to a positive view of your physical sexuality.

1. Begin with a curious mind-set.

2. Locate a mirror that stands up by itself, or any mirror that you can prop up so that both of your hands will be free as you explore your genitals. The magnifying side of a make-up mirror is ideal.

3. Place a towel on the floor or wherever else you can sit comfortably and in good light.

4. As you spread your outer vaginal lips apart, smooth away your pubic hair and look inside your vagina.

5. Drape your inner lips in a variety of ways, noting the different decorative patterns you can create. (Women's inner lips come in all sorts of shapes and textures, all of which are normal and beautiful.)

6. Notice whether your lips are small, medium, large; smooth or textured; dark or light; and symmetrical or asymmetrical. Discover, too, if your inner lips attach at the base or your clitoris, or if they form an arch over the top of your clitoris.

7. Put some K-Y Jelly™ or other water-based lubricant on your finger and stroke your inner lips and notice the sensations you feel.

8. Next, examine your clitoral hood, pulling it back to expose the tip of your clitoris. Notice its shape and size and any difference in color. Stop to marvel at the wonder of this organ, which contains a higher density of nerve

endings even than the glans of the male penis, and serves no other purpose than giving women erotic pleasure.

9. Lightly caress the tip of your clitoris with a lubricated finger and focus on the different sensations you feel. (If you can't see the tip of your clitoris, then place a finger on either side of your clitoral shaft and glide them back and forth to experience erotic sensations.) Stroke, rub or press on your clitoris for a bit and then look carefully to see if its size and color have changed.

10. Now, slowly and gently penetrate your vagina with your finger. (Proceed carefully if you have long nails!) Notice the folds of the vaginal vault and see if you can touch your cervix at the far end.

11. Leaving your finger inside, take a deep breath and relax your hand, arm, all your vaginal muscles, and your anal opening. Take another deep breath, inhaling all the way down to your pelvic floor and let everything go. Take several peaceful moments to savor being inside yourself, loving and appreciating your vagina.

12. Then move your finger to a twelve o'clock position. Use a beckoning motion and observe the sensation. Continue exploring all of your vagina, moving next to the one o'clock position, then two o'clock, and all the way around to the twelve o'clock position. In each position, pay special attention to the sensations you experience and any variations that occur. (Don't be concerned with locating a "G-spot.")

13. By now, your vaginal juices are probably flowing; slowly withdraw your finger and look at your vaginal lubricant. What is it like, clear or milky? With an open, curious mind, sniff it and taste it. Would you describe the taste as salty, neutral, a bit metallic, or in some other way? Is the aroma like yeast, a hint of musk, or something else? Try this on several occasions, so you can get to know how your vagina varies in look, taste, and smell from day to day.

14. Now repeat this process with your lover. Detail each and every part and give it its proper name.

SHAME-CHALLENGING BODYLOVE EXERCISE III
"Making Friends with Your Genitals — for Men"

Men also experience — consciously or unconsciously — shame and guilt over the sexual aspects of their bodies. When was the last time you gave your genitals a thorough exam? The exercise below will help you work through that inhibition.

1. Use a make-up mirror that has a magnifying side.

2. Take a good look at your penis, testicles, and pubic hair pattern from the front, from the side, and even from underneath.

3. Notice the color variations on different parts of your penis and scrotum, the coloring of your pubic hair, and any special identifying "freckles" or other distinguishing features you have that make your genitals uniquely yours.

4. Notice the shape and size of your genitals. Your penis may be wide, narrow, long, short, or, like most men, "medium" in both length and width. Similarly, your testicles have their own special size and shape, and one of them, typically the left, is hanging lower than the other. If you are concerned about size, that's not surprising, since we live in a culture that puts excessive emphasis on it.

5. Examine the head of your penis, the glans. If you are uncircumcised, pull your foreskin back to expose it. How is your glans shaped? Is it shaped like a mushroom, round, or pointed? How would you describe its color?

6. Put a little lubricant (e.g., K-Y Jelly™ or Vaseline™ on your fingers and touch the glans to explore the sensations. Then touch the ridge separating the glans from the shaft (known as the corona). Is the entire ridge equally sensitive, or is there one spot, at the center of the underside, that is the most sensitive? Or is some other portion of the ridge the most sensitive?

7. Now feel your testicles, one at a time; one is usually a bit bigger than the other. They should feel smooth, except for the structure at the back of the testicle that stores sperm, the epididymis.

8. After examining your testicles, gently stroke them to evoke sensations.

9. Then stroke the area directly behind your scrotal sac that extends to your anal opening. You're likely to find this area, the perineum, is also erotically sensitive.

10. Now repeat this process with your lover. Detail each and every part and give it its proper name.

SHAME-CHALLENGING BODYLOVE EXERCISE IV
"Exploring Self-Pleasure — Together"

One way to overcome inhibitions against self-pleasure is to pleasure yourself in front of each other. You can take turns — or do it simultaneously. But at first it's probably best to alternate, with one of you watching the other. The exercise below will guide you sex-cessfully through this process.

Make sure you have privacy and warm, comfortable surroundings.

1. Decide who will begin.

2. Undress.

3. Sit or lie someplace where your lover can see what you are doing clearly.

4. Begin playing with yourself in ways that have brought you the greatest pleasure before.

5. Tell your lover what you are doing and how it feels. If you discover new turn-ons, let your lover know what they are.

6. After you reach orgasm and are feeling relaxed, use your Lovetalk skills to discuss what you each felt and thought.

7. Now watch while your lover self-pleasures himself or herself.

Now that you have begun to undo the damage shame and guilt have done to your capacity for BodyLove, it's time to free yourself from the constraints that concerns over appearance and sexiness place on your erotic connection with your lover. In the next chapter, we'll tackle that issue head-on.

6

HEALTHY IMAGE BODYLOVE
"Giving your lover something beautiful"

"I know I'm not very attractive. I can see that in a mirror. I was a wallflower all through high school and college. Blind dates were about all I got. Now that I'm married, I know my husband loves me. But I still feel ugly when we make love — and that makes me turn him down a lot, even when I'm in the mood. I keep wondering how he can stand to make love to someone as ugly as I."

(Carla, 42)

"I've been complimented on my looks since I was a little girl. Men always found me attractive. I always felt good about that. My boyfriend also tells me how beautiful I am. I enjoy making love with him because I know I am giving him something beautiful."

(Marian, 36)

"My nose is very big. Kids used to make fun of it in school. It made me so self-conscious I don't like to make love with the lights on."

(Cameron, 28)

"I frequently receive compliments on my hair. People say they like it because it's so thick and healthy. To keep these compliments coming in, I get an expensive haircut about every three months. I love it when my husband runs his hands through it. I feel so sexy."

(Lachelle, 31)

For most people, dislike of their appearance is a major barrier to BodyLove. Unless you are one of the fortunate few who fully and unashamedly love your body, concern over looks and desirability cut you off from the full enjoyment of your sexuality — and prevent unleashing the erotic potential of your relationship.

Surveys show most of us consciously and unconsciously compare ourselves to movie stars and the physically perfect specimens showcased in television commercials — making us unhappy with our appearance and convinced others won't find us sexually attractive. Because we aren't "theatrically" beautiful or handsome, we are often reluctant to be seen fully naked by our lovers, to be caressed by them, to make love proudly and to whole-heartedly enjoy the pleasure our lovers are trying to give. No wonder we don't find sex more fun!

We have all grown up in a culture that teaches "what is beautiful is good." Even as a child, your intelligence, potential, and popularity were judged on the basis of your appearance. In turn, without conscious awareness, you learned very quickly to follow suit, and to judge yourself — and later your sexiness — on the same basis.

Books, movies and television consistently harp on this theme/myth: youthful, good looks are needed for good sex. Consequently, if you are among the majority who don't see themselves as sexually attractive, you're likely to feel sexually uncomfortable, self-conscious, unworthy of being loved or being made love to. Some people even become completely turned off sexually by their own fear and feelings of inadequacy.

Consider how you'd react to a movie showing an "ugly" man and an "ugly" woman making love. Or an "elderly" man and "elderly" woman engaging in sexual intercourse. If you're honest, and like most people, your knee-jerk reaction is probably something like "Gross!"

There are many reasons we suffer such anxiety over our body's appearance and attractiveness. We can feel that way because we:

- *compare it negatively* to idealized media images
- *were teased about it* during childhood and adolescence
- *were taught to feel shame* about the body, its parts and/or its functions
- *feel embarrassment* over physical changes, such as pregnancy, illness, injury, weight gain or aging
- *encountered extremely negative feedback* from a lover.

Discovering Your Body's Ability and Attractiveness

How you feel about your body is determined both by how you rate its looks and how well you think it performs physically. People who don't love their bodies over-emphasize the ornamental aspects and devalue the functional aspects. That's why men are far more likely to report satisfaction with their bodies than women. Men place a high value on performance — as well as appearance — and because of sports, athletic activities and gyms, are generally happy with both. Until very recently, women were taught to rate their bodies entirely on their ornamental value — and to discount their functional value. Since few matched the cultural ideals of feminine beauty, the vast majority of women reported discontent with their looks. Whatever your gender, the more you buy into the myth that only a narrow range of physical and facial types defines "beauty" or is to be considered "sexually attractive," the more you are likely to experience dissatisfaction with your body and feel constrained and inadequate during lovemaking.

Women, BodyLove and Appearance: "I have to feel good about my body to be into (sexual activity). If I feel fat, full or haven't worked out in a while, it is hard for me to feel sexy." *(Ruth, 51)* "If I'm feeling flabby, I don't want my lover to see my body; if the lights are too bright, I feel self-conscious." *(Brigette, 32)*

If you're a woman, the social emphasis on "good looks" and "perfect bodies" has profound effects on your sexuality. Forty years ago, Alfred Kinsey's surveys found American women were more reluctant to answer the question "How much do you weigh?" than "How often do you masturbate?" or "Have you ever had a homosexual affair?" Contemporary surveys have revealed that two-thirds of women are still upset about their weight. Worse, the parts of a woman's anatomy considered most erotically stimulating — hips, thighs, stomach, buttocks — are also the very parts of the body that gain weight first, a fact that only creates greater sexual inhibition and self-consciousness. Ultimately, the emphasis on bodily appearance means women are taught to misperceive beauty as the core of their sexuality. Actually, it's the other way around: the active expression of a woman's sexuality makes her beautiful.

Men, BodyLove and Appearance: "I have always known that I was smaller than most men but also know that it is not size, but technique that is more important. I have never wished that my genitals were anything different than what they are." *(Ed, 29)* "Being male, I suppose that we all want our penises to be larger, succumbing to the myth that bigger is better. My defense against this is to be happy and pleased that my apparatus has always worked properly and has been resistant to diseases and other calamities." *(Art, 38)*

If you're a man, feeling your body is unattractive inhibits your losing yourself completely in making love with your lover. The more you worry about how far you deviate from some physical ideal, the more insecure you will be about your desirability. This seems especially true when it comes to penis size. Sadly, just as most women are excessively concerned about their weight, so most men suffer from a deep-seated sense of inferiority over inflated ideas of the "average" penis size — and this seriously impacts on their sexual performance, enjoyment and desire. Some are so self-conscious about size they are reluctant to receive oral sex. This is a particularly needless concern, since performing oral sex on a smaller penis is more pleasurable and comfortable for women. Sexually satisfying a woman — carrying her to heights and depths of passion and sexual fulfillment — has little to do with penis size, anyway. So it's time to give up that obsession and be proud of your genitals — whatever their size.

BODYLOVE SELF-IMAGE EXERCISE I
"Discovering What Your Lover Finds Sexy About Your Body"

Recent research shows that while many of us give our looks a low rating, we are perceived as far more attractive by our lovers. When results are compared, most people were amazed that the physical features they were least happy with were often the very features their lovers found sexiest. The following exercise will help increase your BodyLove quotient by giving you a more balanced — and hence more positive — view of your body and the many ways your lover finds it erotically appealing. (For best results, take it together as a couple and discuss what you learn.)

1. Ask your lover to tell you candidly what he or she likes about your body and what he or she finds sexiest.

2. Make a list of the responses.

3. Examine yourself in a mirror and try to see what it is he or she sees when he or she looks at you.

4. Ask yourself what you have learned from this. Has it changed your perception of any aspect of your body, your attractiveness, allure?

5. Any time you begin feeling unattractive or unsure of your sexiness, mentally review all this positive feedback.

BODYLOVE SELF-IMAGE EXERCISE II
"Learning to Appreciate Your Body Type"

Now that you've discovered that your lover finds aspects of your bodily appearance both attractive and sexy, you're ready to take the next step and learn to truly appreciate your own body. Impossible as this seems, the exercise below will help you overcome your negative physical self-image and learn to feel and believe what others see — that you are an individual possessing strong physical charms and allure.

1. Collect pictures of people you find sexy who represent your particular body type, as well as your particular race or ethnic heritage.

2. Post these pictures in a conspicuous place in your bedroom, on your closet door, or in your bathroom.

3. Look at them once each day to deepen your realization of the similarities between them and yourself.

4. As you drive to work, walk through a mall, or stand in lines, take notice of attractive people you see who share your body type and ethnic background. (You will be surprised at how many there are.)

5. Look at yourself in the mirror. Try to focus in on the parts of your body or carriage that are like theirs.

BODYLOVE SELF-IMAGE EXERCISE III
"Dialog with Your Body"

One way to develop a positive image of your body's appearance and sexiness is to write a dialog with a part or characteristic of your body you have always considered a "flaw." This is a clever way of enabling you, on your own, to see one aspect of your body from an objective, more positive perspective. The effect is akin to the kind of feedback you'd get from a hired consultant, but a lot less expensive and more convenient! Your "flaw" can be anything about your body that you don't like — your crooked nose, the size or shape of your genitals or breasts, your weight, your height.

You may feel a bit awkward at first, but if you're like most, you'll be amazed at how quickly and unself-consciously the dialogue will begin to flow. Writing this kind of dialogue helps you put your "flaw" into perspective and develop constructive suggestions for minimizing your concern.

1. Get a pen and paper or open a file on a word processing program.

2. Write a brief orienting paragraph describing your feelings about a physical feature you have always believed helped make you unattractive — and how this has impacted your sexuality. Sample: *"I've been feeling frustrated about my breasts in the last couple of years and have increasingly worn padded bras. When I was younger it seemed more acceptable to be smaller. Now that I'm an adult (twenty-seven), I'd like to look like one."*

Now write down whatever you would like to say to the physical feature. *Me: This conversation will not be easy because you two really annoy me.*

Write what you imagine this physical feature might say in its own defense. *Breasts: We annoy you? How could an area of your own body be annoying?*

Continue alternating writing what you would like to say to that feature and what it might say in return:

Me: Because I feel cheated — ripped off. Most women have curves and I look like a young boy.

Breasts: Honestly, how many times have you been mistaken for a boy?

Me: I guess the real issue is that I think that bigger breasts would be so much sexier. Most men do not get excited looking at flat-chested women in bikinis. I'm tired of looking like a pre-pubescent schoolgirl.

Breasts: I see. So you're trying to attract the kind of men who watch "Baywatch"?

Me: No. That's not it either. I just know that the majority of men prefer large breasts.

Breasts: Oh please. Name one boyfriend who seemed unhappy with your breasts. Not only that, but think about the kind of men you've dated. Do you think any of them were lying to you about their preference for small breasts? Believe it or not, some men do prefer them.

Me: I believed them at the time, but I always wonder if they were just being kind or if they would've been even more pleased if you were just a little bigger...

Breasts: So you think that men would be more pleased with you and find you more exciting if we were larger? Consider how it would affect your life if you had large breasts.

Me: Some men might find me sexier and I'd look better in bikinis and sweaters. I could wear leotards to the gym instead of T-shirts.

Breasts: Anything else?

Me: I think some people feel sorry for me. Like I am deficient or handicapped or something.

Breasts: How does that make you feel?

Me: As if I am inadequate somehow.

Breasts: Do you think you are?

Me: Actually no. I've always felt sexy with the men I've been with.

Breasts: In fact, you've had lots of positive things to say about us in the past.

Me: That's true. I like the idea that I appear streamlined. I feel like I am very light and lithe, and it helps me in my sports. Not only that, but I can wear simple dresses and look elegant.

Breasts: And don't forget how you don't have to put up with bra straps digging into your shoulders that your friend Monica complains about.

Me: I'd forgotten about that.

Breasts: It sounds like you sway too easily to the ideals that movies and magazines market to you.

Me: You're right. That's so much junk. This was really good for me. I'd forgotten all the positives and I feel a whole lot better about how I look.

Follow through by repeating your new found insights whenever you find yourself beginning to feel unhappy with that feature again.

It's difficult to feel completely comfortable making love unless you have confidence in your own sex appeal. The final chapter of the BodyLove section will help you to find that confidence. You can begin to see yourself as desirable through your lover's eyes!

7

SEX APPEAL BODYLOVE
"When my lover wears.....
I can't control myself"

"I find my lover very sexy when he wears his glasses and clothing that makes him look very intellectual. Or when he only covers the bottom part of his body, baring his masculine chest."   (Dottie, 43)

"What I find sexy and alluring on my wife is when she shows some cleavage. She has nice breasts and it is really a turn on for me when she shows a little bit of them off in an attractive party dress."

(Geraldo, 38)

"When my lover wears jeans without a shirt on, I can't control myself. Jeans always seem to fit his butt perfectly, and I like it even more if he is barefoot. He seems more carefree and relaxed dressed like this."   (Debbie, 34)

"I prefer a little conservativeness, but I admit I like clothes that reveal her curves."   (Philip, 30)

All of us want to appear sexy in the eyes of our lovers. Feeling your body is sexy, being proud of it and wanting to share that sexiness with your lover is fundamental to hot lovemaking. But if your body doesn't feel sexy to you, you can't project "sexy" for your lover.

However, no matter how you rate your own sexiness, you can make yourself appear even more alluring by dressing and grooming in ways that show off your positive features. Heightening your sex appeal makes you feel more alive, stimulating, eager to enjoy the delights of lovemaking, and sexy. It is also the capstone of BodyLove.

Dressing sexy means feeling sexy: "I feel very good whenever I dress in a sexy and alluring way. When I don't have any hang-ups about the way I look, I can concentrate more on my lover." *(Annie, 36)* "I feel confident about myself when I dress in a sexy way. It makes me feel like everyone is admiring me." *(Richard, 24)* "Dressing sexy makes me feel beautiful. I feel very feminine and more confident than usual. It's a real ego-booster." *(Brenda, 27)* "I feel great when I'm dressed sexy. I not only dress sexy for my lover, I dress sexy for myself. I feel good when I think I look good." *(Leah, 32)*

There's more to a healthy sexual relationship than what you wear. But it can add an important dash of seasoning to your lovelife. This is especially true in long term relationships when people begin taking each other for granted, forgetting the allure that sexy grooming and dressing added to their sex life in the early days.

The importance of dressing sexy: "I believe dressing sexy has a great effect on your sexual life with your lover. Dressing sexy gives your lover something to fantasize about in public surroundings." *(Sara, 28)* "I think that my lover's sexy style of dress reveals a lot and in essence appeals to me. I find myself being very aroused by her and wanting to have sex with her more. It adds a little flavor and flare." *(Bill, 36)*

"When my lover dresses in a sexy way, I become extremely wet and aroused! I become more aggressive and take more control and express my wants and desires to him. Our sexual encounter is always more enjoyable and he likes it when I'm more active than passive in our sexual activities." *(Darla, 39)* "Dressing sexy can be a form of foreplay. And there's nothing that could enhance sex like good foreplay." *(Jose, 28)*

Spicing Appeal with Sexy Underwear

Boosting sex appeal doesn't stop with "outerwear." What you wear underneath can make a big difference in how you feel about your body's sexiness. It also sends an unmistakable signal to your lover about how you feel about him and the sexual bond between you.

Believe it or not, surveys show that there is a correlation between the kind of underwear couples choose and the sexual health of their relationship. People who consistently don functional, drab or worn-out underwear generally report negative feelings about their own sexuality and reluctance to engage in sex. Those who consistently wear attractive, sexy lingerie or men's briefs report positive feelings about their own erotic appeal and about lovemaking.

The timeless appeal of sexy undergarments: "I wear silk boxers whenever I go on a date because girls really like silk and how it feels. Also silk, satin or lace panties and bras on girls make me horny too." *(Sam, 25)*

How it makes the wearer feel: "When I wear sexy underwear, I feel very sexy. It's funny because no one else knows that I am wearing them, but as long as I do, it makes me feel good about how I look." *(Lillian, 54)* "I consider boxers 'sexy.' I wear them a lot, particularly when my wife and I are doing something special. They make me feel sexier." *(Mel, 42)* "Regardless of how I look on the outside — bad hair day, sweats, jeans — if I have on sexy underwear I feel as if I have a secret." *(Elisha, 28)*

How it makes the lover feel: "It definitely adds excitement when I know my lover is wearing something underneath that is sexy. It's like opening a present." *(Jerry, 39)* "I like it when I see my boyfriend in one of those men's bikini-like pouches — and nothing else. Seeing it bulging under there really gets me excited." *(Carol, 31)* "I love it when he dresses up for me or when he wears his Calvin Klein underwear. I start to think about what I'm going to do to him in bed later that night." *(Meg, 36)*

BODYLOVE SEX APPEAL EXERCISE I
"Exploring What You Find Sexy on You and Your Lover"

If you've been together long, you probably already have some idea what you wear that turns your lover on. It's equally likely you've shared some of your own feelings with your lover. But due to inhibitions we all share about discussing sexual matters, whatever exchanges and hints you've shared about the subject have probably been incomplete and fragmented. They may even be outdated as tastes change and so do our bodies. (If you've been working on LoveSkill #1, LoveTalk, you're on your way to overcoming these inhibitions.)

Do the following exercise as a couple if possible. If not, try it on your own. You'll gain a new appreciation of the role sexy, provocative dressing plays in your own lovelife. It will also trigger multiple inspirations on how you can significantly enhance your sex appeal.

Write or type out your answers to the following questions. Answer as fully and in as much detail as you can.

1. How do you feel about the idea of dressing in a sexy, alluring manner?

2. What would you consider a "sexy" way of dressing for yourself?

3. How do you feel when dressed this way?

4. What concerns, if any, do you have about dressing like this?

5. What apparel do you consider "sexy" on your lover?

6. How do you feel about your lover dressing in this way?

7. If you could ask your lover to wear one very special thing for you — what would it be?

8. Why would this turn you on?

9. What effect do you believe your dressing in a sexy, alluring way has on your lovemaking afterward?

10. What effect do you believe your lover's dressing in a sexy way has on the quality of your lovemaking afterward?

Now share your answers with each other. Discuss those answers and then plan together to incorporate more erotically enticing clothing into your lovelife.

BODYLOVE SEX APPEAL EXERCISE II
"Wearing What Your Lover Finds Sensual and Alluring"

Here's a simple technique that guarantees what you're wearing will fire each other's passions.

1. Ask your lover to accompany you on a shopping expedition and help you pick sexy clothes that would turn her on to see you wear (determine in advance what your budget can afford). Or ask her to surprise you with a sexy gift or underwear.

2. While shopping, ask your lover if she'd be willing to have you return the favor and select a sexy item for her.

3. Plan an evening out for which you each get to pick how the other dresses.

BODYLOVE SEX APPEAL EXERCISE III
"Trying on Sexy Lingerie and Briefs"

If you still feel a bit inhibited about donning or viewing your lover in sexy underwear, this couples exercise, developed by my friend Jean Marie Stine, will help you become comfortable. In addition, it provides a delightful way of setting the stage for amorous fulfillment later in the evening.

1. Pick an evening when you can be home alone and undisturbed.

2. Each of you should purchase three pairs of the kinds of underwear you know your lover finds sexy (these do not have to be expensive).

3. After a pleasant dinner, flip a coin. The winner retires to a different room and dons one of the items (or a set of items) of underwear.

4A. This person then returns to the main room and gives the other person a "fashion show."

4B. Alternatively, you could put the lingerie — men's briefs or whatever — on underneath outer clothing and perform a "striptease."

5. This should continue until all the new clothing has been worn.

6. Then it is the other person's turn to model the underwear.

7. Each of you should keep on the final items.

8. Having turned each other on visually, if you are both aroused and agreeable, let your erotic inclinations take it from there.

Once you and your lover have become truly comfortable with your bodies, you are ready to explore the potent realm of LoveTouch.

Love Skill Three:
Love Touch

8

SEX-CESSFUL LOVETOUCH
"The most special and tender part of our intimacy"

"My lover's touch is the emotional and sexual bond I share with her." (Brian, 38)

"LoveTouch is the most special and tender part of our intimacy. Even though my boyfriend and I have been together a long time, I still quiver when he touches me." (Candice, 27)

"Touching is very important to me. I am a very affectionate person and enjoy being in physical contact with my lover." (Glen, 42)

"The touching that goes on in my relationship is usually reassuring or warm and compassionate, depending on the situation."
(Bonnie, 33)

"If there is something there could be more of, it would be her touching me both affectionately and erotically. It is one of the great pleasures of life — never enough." (Seth, 24)

Once you feel comfortable with discussing sexual issues, as well as with your own and your lover's body, it's time to discover the power of touch to communicate love, create intimacy and fire passion.

A smile is nice. So is good conversation and an approving look. But when the chips are down, it's LoveTouch we crave. Skin on skin. That's where we begin, and where we end. Touching — and plenty of it — is one of the fundamental building blocks of a sex-cessful relationship.

As James Vaughan writes in *The Monogamy Myth: Surviving Affairs*, "We can change our lives and the lives of those around us by reaching out and touching." It's touching that tells us most clearly where we stand with another person.

Touch is the first sense you develop as an embryo. It is the "mother of the senses." Our sense of touch is the largest sense "organ," with millions of tactile receptors located throughout the entire body.

LoveTouch is important to your personal well-being and to the health of your relationship. Lovers have an absolute hunger for touching. LoveTouch dissolves barriers and establishes connection with your lover.

Over and over, studies have proved that frequent touching during infancy and childhood — and adulthood — is absolutely essential for healthy emotional growth and development — including sexual development. Children who are fed, clothed, and sheltered, but not otherwise touched or held, grow up emotionally stunted, with severe psychological problems. Research has shown that lack of adequate touching can even kill infants; it's known as "failure-to-thrive" syndrome. On the other hand, touching alone can be a source of psychological comfort and physical healing. Hospital patients who are often touched by the nursing staff recover more quickly and are discharged sooner.

Our early experiences with touching even help determine our capacity both to give and to receive love. Writes anthropologist Ashley Montagu:

"By being stroked, and caressed, and carried, and cuddled, comforted, and cooed to, by being loved, (you learn) to stroke and caress and cuddle, comfort and coo, and to love others.

"In this sense love is sexual in the healthiest sense of that word. It implies involvement, concern, responsibility, tenderness, and awareness of the needs, sensibilities, and vulnerabilities of the other. All this is communicated to (you) through the skin in the early months of (your) life... "

LoveTouch: The Forgotten Language

Touching is the most basic and powerful language for communicating comfort, care, affection, pleasure and passion. LoveTouch affirms and deepens the connection with your lover. LoveTouch — to express your many moods and feelings — should be fun.

But sadly, our Puritan heritage has made LoveTouch a forgotten language — and taken the fun out of it — for too many of us. People from Greece and Italy and similar countries, where touching is common, see people from "noncontact" cultures — e.g., England, Germany, and much of America — as cold and unfeeling.

In many typical "mainstream" American homes (like yours?) affectionate touching is all too rare. What touching you do see is often an initiation of sex. This is particularly true for men. Many men have no model of non-sexual touching. They've often had almost no physical contact with their fathers, particularly after they have reached a "certain" age — typically preteen. If a boy's father ever did kiss him or hold him, that usually stopped abruptly around age nine or ten.

Girls are more likely to be touched by their parents even as they enter adolescence. But there are many homes in which kissing, hugging or other displays of affection are absent — between parents and children, and even between parent and parent.

If one lover finds initiating affectionate contact difficult, the other may feel starved for nonsexual touching and resent its absence. When these lovers do agree to lovemaking, it's not because they want sex, but because they are "touch hungry." Typically, the attempt to substitute sexual touching for affectionate touching is not deeply satisfying, and lovers are left feeling empty or alienated.

When a person is uncomfortable with affectionate touching, the urge for sex is often an unwitting substitute for emotional closeness. As you'll see in the following sections, several forms of LoveTouch, not merely sexual, play important roles in your relationship and form the "glue" that bonds you to your lover.

Affectionate, Sensual and Sexual LoveTouch

From infancy on, touch is a source of great sensual as well as sexual pleasure. While you probably don't recall it, as a baby you almost surely delighted in sensations of the skin. If you were typical, you experienced the pleasures of being bathed, hugged, caressed, tickled. And if you were typical, you also touched yourself throughout your body, even fondling your genitals.

Encompassed in the above experiences are the three major kinds of touching: *affectionate LoveTouch, sensual LoveTouch,* and *sexual LoveTouch.*

Without all three, no human being or relationship can be complete and healthy. Together, they have the capacity to increase your sense of trust, your willingness to be intimate and vulnerable and to create a deep sense of "good will" toward your lover.

Each kind of LoveTouch makes a specific contribution to the strength and vitality of your relationship. *Affectionate LoveTouch* provides comfort and security. *Sensual LoveTouch* provides pleasure and relaxation. *Sexual LoveTouch* fuels passion and dissolves barriers.

Through LoveTouch, couples express all the vital components of their love for each other — caring, attachment, intimacy, passion and pleasure. Your relationship rests on a solid foundation when all three forms of LoveTouch are a constant and ongoing part of your lives together.

Lovers in sex-cessful relationships constantly show their love for each other by touching each other in all three ways. When any one is missing, it throws a sexual relationship out of balance.

When even one is missing, it's a warning sign that something is amiss. When lovers start to become hostile, resentful, angry, or mistrustful, the urge to touch is the first to go.

Lack of Affectionate LoveTouch: Sex-cessful touching begins with affectionate LoveTouch. When lovers don't touch each other affectionately, the fundamental sense of tenderness and nurturance that it provides is lost. Even — or especially — when sexual touching is present, you are likely to feel unloved, reduced to a "sex object" and resentful. In addition, the extreme sense of emotional deprivation resulting from lack of affectionate touching will prevent you from continuing to be sexual in the long run.

Lack of Sensual LoveTouch: When sensual LoveTouch is missing, desire during sex is also missing. Lack of sensual touch is the difference between bad sex and good sex — as well as the difference between good sex and sublime sex.

It's sensual touch that makes sex *sexy*. Without it, you run the risk of sex that is boring and merely functional, making you a prime candidate for lack of desire. Without it, you lose out on a very powerful turn-on. Without its relaxing effects, you're more likely to experience anxiety — and that deadens arousal. Men who proceed directly to sexual LoveTouch may experience erection difficulties; women may have trouble reaching orgasm (many women say they are orgasmic only when both sensual and sexual LoveTouch are present).

Lack of Sexual LoveTouch: Sexual LoveTouch gives lovers a fundamental validation of their attractiveness as sexual beings. It is an affirmation of your masculinity or femininity. No amount of affectionate LoveTouch can give you this validation.

Lovers who only touch affectionately are primarily companions, not lovers. You're likely to feel more like roommates or sister and brother. You may well feel loved, but not in the special way sought in an intimate relationship.

While it's possible you both find this acceptable, it's not likely. Instead, your relationship may seem superficially stable. You may not have overt conflicts. You may even continue the same way for years. But it's likely you also feel quietly discontented and in a rut. When the opportune moment presents itself, or when one of you is suddenly swept away by an unexpected romantic encounter, your "stable" relationship evaporates.

More typically, lovers who want sexual LoveTouch but do not receive it experience acute deprivation and distress. The lover who desires erotic contact feels rejected, unloved or — worse — unattractive. Her sense of self-esteem is injured, and she feels either undeserving or that something is wrong with her.

SEX-CESSFUL LOVETOUCH EXERCISE
"How Healthy Is LoveTouch In Your Relationship?"

Put an "x" before any question you can say "yes" to.

Do you have a sense of "touching hunger" in your relationship?

Do you feel rebuffed by your lover when you touch him or her affectionately? Sensually? Sexually?

Do you believe your lover misinterprets your touching?

During sexual activity, are you bothered by performance concerns?

Do you and your lover have disagreements about touching?

Do you settle for one kind of touching when you really want another?

Do you or your lover lack interest in sexual touching?

Affirmative answers to one or more these questions suggests a lack of — or an imbalance between — affectionate, sensual and sexual touching that may be adversely affecting your relationship.

In the following three chapters we'll be taking a closer look at each of these forms of touch —*affectionate, sensual* and *sexual* — and how you can optimize the touching in your own loving relationship.

9

AFFECTIONATE LOVETOUCH
"Feeling loved, alive, happy and cared for"

"If touching is genuinely affectionate, it relaxes me, allows me to be more spontaneous and open. Makes me feel accepted, wanted."

(Emilio, 27)

"It feels especially good if I've had a hard day, or am feeling down."

(Chuck, 52)

"Affectionate LoveTouch makes me feel very loved, alive, happy and cared for."

(Lucille, 54)

"I love it when he affectionately touches me like a hug or an affectionate kiss, or when we rub noses."

(Natalya, 30)

"I like to be touched affectionately at all times. I like anything from a short hand squeeze to a long, affectionate and caring hug. Of course, hugs are my favorite."

(Sarah, 27)

"I like to be cuddled and hugged and just a simple touching means so much to me. I like affection continuously and whenever we are together."

(Vince, 34)

Affectionate LoveTouch is fun. It's the spark that lights the fire of sex-cessful loving. Affectionate LoveTouch creates the physical bonding in a relationship. It communicates the key elements of intimacy:

Warmth
Caring
Support
Reassurance
Connection

No matter what the situation — from grief or fear to gratitude and joy — almost everyone agrees the one reaction that satisfies them most is a friendly, sympathetic touch. Scientific studies have found couples whose relationships were working engaged in significantly more LoveTouch, while those in troubled relationships rarely reached out affectionately to each other.

Affectionate LoveTouch between lovers seems so natural you would think it was inevitable. At the beginning of a relationship we touch each other frequently with affection and caring. We hug, caress, pat, brush up against one another, and simply reach out in reassurance.

We enjoy affectionate LoveTouch and have a lot of fun doing it. But sooner or later, we begin taking the connection for granted. Eventually, we almost all find ourselves touching less frequently. And not surprisingly, we discover the fun is gone out of the relationship with it.

Why does the amount of touch — and the closeness it engenders — almost inevitably leak out of our lives? One answer is that cultural, familial, and gender-based inhibitions about touching — and especially affectionate touching — practically guarantee that unless we work at it, our impulse to share affection via physical contact is doomed from the start.

The situation is further complicated when you and your lover attach different meanings to affectionate touching. Many cultural heritages not only discourage touching, they guarantee trouble for lovers by giving men and women completely different guidelines about when affectionate touching is appropriate. The resultant gender gap makes touching a constant source of friction for many couples.

Men, Women & Affectionate LoveTouch

Clearly, men and women attach different meaning to LoveTouch. Men tend to restrict LoveTouch to sexual situations. Women expect and need it to maintain the true feeling of closeness and emotional contact that are crucial to a relationship's sex-cess.

Women and Affectionate LoveTouch: "Touching is very important to me; especially when there is no expectation of sex." *(Francesca, 36)*

If you're a woman, you're far more likely to have experienced affectionate touching during childhood. This is particularly true of same-sex affectionate touching with friends and relatives. Consequently, you're more accustomed to the use of touching to express caring and more likely expect it, both from friends *and* in your relationship!

If you're a woman, you're far more likely to expect a lover to use affectionate touching as a "natural" way to express love for you. You're also likely to expect it all the more after marriage. "Women," one recent study concluded, "use touching during marriage to preserve the bond." This is at least partly true because whatever sexual innuendo may be read into touching before marriage is, after marriage, completely sanctioned and permissible.

Since the frequency of affectionate LoveTouch often drops after the first year of marriage, this is fertile staging ground for another clash in the battle between the genders. Most women who don't get enough affectionate LoveTouch from their mates complain that, "He only touches me when he wants sex; I feel used."

Men and Affectionate LoveTouch: "I don't feel I have any inhibitions that I am aware of, except for the affectionate touching thing." *(Leon, 36)* "It's hard for me to do affectionate touching." *(Rich, 47)* "If the woman who is touching me is just a friend I get very uncomfortable. I think maybe because I'm a walking hormone." *(Nathan, 21)*

If you're a typical male, you grew up with significant restrictions on touching. Embracing, caressing and other displays of affectionate touching were discouraged as "unmanly" when you were a child. Later they were ridiculed as "feminine" or "mushy." This is to be expected, since in our culture only women are supposed to express tender feelings openly.

The only form of touching other males encouraged was touching women for sexual purposes. Like many men, you may think of touching primarily as a way of initiating sex, a necessity to be "put up with" if you are to arouse a lover. More significantly, for the long-term survival of your relationship — and the satisfaction of your lover — you may only be comfortable with sexual touching and find other forms difficult.

Fortunately, while gender differences over the need for affectionate LoveTouch exist, they can be transcended. Many men have made the effort to rid themselves of the traditional male barriers to affectionate touching. As one male told me of his relationship: "We have no barriers with affectionate touching. I think that's our favorite kind of touching because we both feel good that we're there for each other and aren't feeling pressured into having sex or anything."

For all that we differ on giving and receiving affectionate touch, the forms men and women like most are remarkably similar, as the following chart shows.

MEN	WOMEN
A long hug after a long day	Arm over shoulder
A kiss on the cheek	Neck and chest caresses
Hand holding	Touching lips with finger
Stroking my hair	Holding hands
Touching my face	Touching my breasts
Scratching my chest	Fingers through my hair
Caressing my back	Rubbing my shoulders
Rubbing my arms, feet, body	Putting hand on my leg while driving
Tickling my stomach, chest and nipples	Rubbing noses
Laying my head on my lover's lap	Little affectionate kisses (lips just softly touching)
Feeling genitals /neck/ back/foot	Nibbling my ear
	Snuggling
	Stroking arm
	Caressing buttocks and thighs
	Foot/neck/face/back massages

Differences in temperament and personality can also inhibit our urge to touch. People who are comfortable with affectionate LoveTouch are likely to share a number of traits: mentally flexible; talkative, cheerful; socially dominant; satisfied with physical appearance and body; less anxious about life; less suspicious of other people's motives.

People who experience difficulty with Affectionate LoveTouch generally possess one or more negative personality traits: rigid, authoritarian and controlling; socially withdrawn; difficulty expressing feelings; low self-esteem; emotionally unstable.

If your upbringing, gender or personality are putting a crimp in your affectionate touching, don't despair. You can change traits you're ready to shed, if you're willing to *practice* the new behaviors you want. Changes in your feelings and perceptions will follow in time. Such changes don't come easily or quickly, but you'll be well rewarded for persistent effort!

Before the Eyes of the World

Conflicts can also arise over public displays of affection through touching. Some people don't feel comfortable with any form of public affection, not even holding hands or a simple hug. Others enjoy affectionate touching in public, feeling that it reinforces and deepens the bond.

Uncomfortable with public LoveTouch: "I don't feel that public touching is necessary. It doesn't bother me, but I don't think it's necessary to show how one feels. In privacy, I think it's great." *(Muhammed, 36)* "In private I think anything (within limits) is all right. But in public, I prefer to take it a little easy. Hugging and hand-holding are alright, sometimes kissing. But that depends very much on where you are. I know that I sometimes don't like seeing people kissing on the bus or something." *(Jill, 28)* "Affection around friends is not comfortable for me. I would feel as if I were invading their space." *(Grace, 42)* "Touching in public is OK to a small degree. But when it is to the point that it makes others uncomfortable around you, it should be stopped." *(Dave, 34)*

Comfortable with public LoveTouch: "We are always touching when we are together. So in public it's usually real obvious that we are a couple and very much in love with each other." *(April, 36)* "I like showing affection no matter where or when. Unfortunately, my lover is very private. No touching in public." *(Martina, 31)* "I am not concerned about how people look at my lover and me. We kiss hug, whatever... any time we feel like it." *(Terrence, 26)*

AFFECTIONATE LOVETOUCH EXERCISE I
SELF-ASSESSMENT
"What Have You Learned about Affectionate Touching?"

The exercise that follows will help you explore your history with regard to affectionate touching and pinpoint the sources of any inhibition. This process alone may enable you to develop a new perspective.

Pick a specific time and place when you know you'll be able to give each other undivided attention for thirty to sixty minutes. Don't rush the process. You may or may not finish all of the following questions. If you don't finish, simply pick a new time when you can continue where you left off.

Write down your answers to the following questions about your family of origin (growing up). If doing this with a lover, share your answers. Be specific.

Was touching among family members avoided, or encouraged?
Who exactly touched whom?
> *Did everybody touch everybody?*
> *Parents and children only?*
> *Females only?*
> *Siblings only?*

On what occasions did affectionate touching occur?
What kind of affectionate touching did you see between your parents?
How often?
What were the messages given to you about affectionate touching:
> *Among family members?*
> *Among same-sex friends?*
> *Among opposite-sex friends?*

How did you feel about your family's pattern of affectionate touching?
> *Is it one you were comfortable with?*
> *How would you have wanted it to be different?*

Was there any abusive touching in your family — or did you experience any elsewhere when you were growing up? (If so, you may wish to seek the guidance of a competent trained therapist who can help you deal with the implications of that unfortunate experience for the development of your own Love Skills.)

AFFECTIONATE LOVETOUCH EXERCISE II
"Reinforcing Your Caring, Love & Commitment"

Sharing your views about some key aspects of affectionate touching can help you and your lover better understand each other, learn each other's preferences, and jointly agree on ways to strengthen your relationship through LoveTouch. The bottom line is to communicate openly about what kind of physical contact means caring and affection to you. And to describe those that make either you or your partner feel uncomfortable or exploited.

Again, write out your answers before discussing them. You will feel less inhibited about expressing your likes and dislikes. And, as always, be specific.

What bearing does your family's pattern of affectionate touching have on you now?

What kinds of affectionate touching do you like most?

What kinds of affectionate touching do you like least?

How does affectionate touching make you feel about yourself?

About your lover?

When is affectionate touching most important to you?

Which kinds of affectionate touching are you comfortable with in public, if any?

Which are you uncomfortable with?

How do you feel if your affectionate touch gets no response?

How do you feel if your partner touches you and you choose not to respond?

How satisfied are you with the amount and type of affectionate touching you receive in your relationship?

What changes, if any, would you like? (Be very specific.)

Which of these changes, if any, would mean the most to you? (Why?)

What change are you willing to make now with regard to the amount of affectionate touching you give?

What change would you be willing to make in the future?

AFFECTIONATE LOVETOUCH EXERCISE III
"Reinforcing Your Caring, Love & Commitment"

Once you've answered these last questions, it's time to make a commitment to change (unless things are perfect already!). Look at the list of ways your lover would like to see your affection expressed. Consciously decide to add one behavior to your repertoire each week. Even if you initially feel a bit awkward, go for it. Giving the one you love the kind of affectionate LoveTouch he or she wants will reignite the spark in your relationship.

Remember especially the principles of "baby steps," risking, and the goal of *enhancement, not perfection.* A little bit of awkwardness or anxiety is common whenever you make changes.

Also, be sure to praise and compliment your lover for any efforts to meet your needs for affectionate LoveTouch. The rewards for you both will be worth it!

Now that you have recaptured the sense of closeness, intimacy and trust affectionate touching engenders, it's time to take the next step and enter the heady, erotic realm of sensual LoveTouch.

10

SENSUAL LOVETOUCH
"Love's silent messenger"

"Sensual LoveTouching is the most effective way to show me that my lover cares."   (Hideo, 22)

"Sensual LoveTouch is a loving expression on the part of my lover, taking pleasure in pleasing me."   (Peggy, 43)

"In my relationships sensual LoveTouching has been the silent messenger. It has told my lover how much I want him... and it told him that I cared without any words."   (Amber, 32)

"Sensual LoveTouch relaxes me, soothes, turns me on, makes me feel loving."   (Paul, 31)

"I get very turned on when I'm caressed. I close my eyes and really feel everything."   (Gloria, 52)

"Sensual LoveTouching makes me feel sexy and assertive. I feel very powerful when I touch and am being touched in a sensual way. I also feel relaxed and dreamy. Wow! Lots of emotions, huh?"

(Gayle, 29)

When affectionate LoveTouch has brought the two of you close in the warmth of intimacy and caring, sensual caresses can kindle that warmth into passion and desire.

Sensuality is the celebration of the body and its ability to give us pleasure. Whether it's sensual LoveTouch or savoring a wonderful meal, sensuality results from being fully absorbed and focused on our moment-by-moment experience. It involves slowing down and "smelling the roses."

As the Phantom of the Opera sang so mellifluously to Christine in "The Music of the Night": "...*floating, falling, sweet intoxication; Touch me, trust me, savor each sensation...*" and continues with "...*Softly, deftly, music shall caress you. Hear it, feel it, secretly possess you; Open up your mind...*"

THAT is what sensuality is all about; the Phantom was beseeching Christine to become fully absorbed in the here-and-now sensuality of sound. The sensuality of touch, because it involves two bodies literally touching each other, may be even more profound.

Sensual LoveTouch is a building block of erotic fun and sex-cessful relationships. Because it is unhurried and non-goal oriented, you and your lover are likely to experience it as a particularly strong way to express deep caring for one another.

No other form of communication is more intimate or produces such a sense of trust and surrender between lovers. It is truly a very special gift only the two of you can share together.

Is Sensual Touch Just an Appetizer?
Sensual LoveTouch can be so satisfying you simply want to melt into the sensations and float away, without thinking of sexual LoveTouch. As one woman put it:

"I think sensual LoveTouching is a gift from the gods. To be able to express your emotions of bliss through the tactile experience is wonderful. I believe these are intimate moments of ecstasy that are solely shared with your lover and don't include sexual activity in the classic sense of intercourse, orgasm..."

Paradoxically, sensual LoveTouch simultaneously relaxes and stimulates you.

Because sensual LoveTouch is such a source of pure physical comfort and pleasure, it often produces a languorous sense of bliss, well-being and harmony. The sweet sensations draw you irresistibly away from outer distractions.

When physical pleasure becomes so intense, it can be an end in itself, or it can be a turn-on — an erotic prelude to sexual LoveTouch and physical intimacy.

It's through sensual LoveTouch that a sense of mutual relaxation, a lowering of barriers, a feeling of spontaneous intimacy is created between lovers. Sensual LoveTouch is an irreplaceable way to communicate with your lover on a rich, deep level of surrender to each other and the moment. It is a way to embrace the pleasure you and your lover can experience together through something as simple as a sensuous touch.

As you prepare for sensual LoveTouch, remember the focus is on awakening you and your lover to the incredible harmony, peace and pleasure you can bring to each other. The focus is not on the genitals and the aim is not sexual arousal, even though this may occur. And if it should, you'll gain the most from these exercises if you contain your *sexual* energy until after the exercise is over.

It's Not Always Easy

At first, you may feel uncomfortable about giving or receiving sensual LoveTouch. Nearly everyone was taught not to indulge in pure sensual pleasure for its own sake. Getting into sensual LoveTouch requires letting go of the basic idea that the "pleasures of the flesh" are sinful.

As a male, you may not see the point of sensual LoveTouch at first. Men are supposed to do things that have purpose. You've been taught you're supposed to "succeed" — the faster, the better — whether it's making your first million or "scoring" sexually. Consequently, you may not see any point to sensual LoveTouch; it doesn't seem to go anywhere and it's not about speed. Or you may be uncomfortable for fear you'll be inexperienced and unaccomplished (still another way of not living up to the masculine image).

Women often have reason to be suspicious that sensual LoveTouch is just another ploy designed to prime them for sex. And some women have deeply ambivalent or negative feelings about touching because they experienced abusive touching at some point in their lives. Unless a woman trusts that her lover is not attempting to seduce her with sensual LoveTouch, that he has no ulterior motives beyond expressing his caring, she is likely to feel strong resistance to the idea.

Any of the issues raised here can be good reasons for the two of you to agree not to have full sexual intercourse after your first few "practice sessions" of sensual LoveTouch, no matter how aroused you both may become.

The "Giver" and the "Receiver"

During sessions of sensual LoveTouch, one lover should be the "giver," and one the "receiver." You should take turns being each.

Sticking to these roles may need a bit of getting used to at first — especially that of the receiver. Both men and women have been raised to be givers and not receivers.

• *Men and receiving sensual LoveTouch:* If you're a man, you're likely to feel more comfortable as a giver because it's part of the image of "man as action-oriented doer." But it's important that you learn to enjoy relaxing and receiving the delicious sensations and pleasures your lover will be creating. Don't try to reciprocate. Instead, let yourself experience the wonderful healing power of being cherished for your very being — not because of how you "perform" or what you've accomplished.

• *Women and receiving sensual LoveTouch:* If you're a woman, you too may initially feel uncomfortable as the receiver. Being nurtured runs counter to your socialization to be the nurturer. You may feel it's selfish to receive so much pleasure.

• *Intimacy, bonding and sensual LoveTouch:* As the receiver, whether you're a man or woman, allow yourself to accept the rewards of sensual LoveTouch — sensual LoveTouch both calls for and creates surrender and trust — to fully become immersed in the melting pleasure you will experience.

As the giver, stay fully focused in the present moment. Steep yourself in the pleasurable sensations you are experiencing in this role. Let yourself experience the fascination of learning more and more each time about your lover's body, as you develop an intimate knowledge of it.

As the giver, let your hands be extensions of your feelings as you caress your lover. Let them particularly express your caring and your love. Use your eyes, ears and hands to tune in on your lover's responses. Facial expressions, body movements and sound are vital clues as to when your sensuous LoveTouch is going right. You'll begin to learn where to touch your lover to evoke the deepest sighs of pleasure and comfort.

After a few minutes, you'll both find you're relaxing and getting in tune with one another. Rapport, a non-verbal sense of intimacy, harmony and communication, will begin to develop between you: the giver's touch responds to the receiver's signals and the receiver's reactions respond to the giver's touch.

The experience becomes richly rewarding for you, regardless of which role, giver or receiver, you are in. You may not want to disrupt the nonverbal flow of this intimate experience — even with LoveTalk. (But do speak up if something hurts or makes you feel uncomfortable!)

Guidelines for Sensual LoveTouch Sessions

Once you discover the deep rewards of sensual LoveTouch, you're likely to find it so satisfying you make it a part of your life.

• *Engage in sensual LoveTouch whenever you both feel like it.* (Keep a reasonable sense of your surroundings, of course.) Sensual LoveTouch can be spontaneous or planned. Planned versus spontaneous: At first, planned sensual LoveTouch sessions are best. You'll be less concerned about being interrupted or distracted and find it easier to give yourself up to the experience. Planning could be as simple as an unspoken understanding sensual LoveTouch sessions will take place Saturday evenings after dinner, or on Sunday afternoons. Later, after you have really gotten the idea of sensual LoveTouch, sessions can become more spontaneous — sparked by the mood.

• *Never rush:* But never rush it. Typically, a sensuous LoveTouch exercise takes about thirty minutes. Since many audio tapes are also that long, you may want to include music as background to your session. Or, set a noiseless timer. (But if you're the giver, don't watch the clock!)

• *Decide in advance: Sex or no sex?* Do you want your sensual LoveTouch exercise to end in lovemaking? If most LoveTouch in the past led to sexual activity, you may want some space to learn to enjoy sensual LoveTouch without feeling pressured for sex. My suggestion? Allow yourself two or three sessions with no sex. After that, go with what feels right *for both of you.* Communicate about this clearly with your lover. If you've agreed not to proceed to sexual activity, stick to it. Resist the temptation to further act on those feelings. This is how you learn to truly savor each sensation and maximize pleasure.

• *Decide in advance. Fixed rule or shifting roles?* Do you expect to shift roles when you do these exercises? If one of you is feeling particularly down or tired, you might wish to concentrate only on giving to that person.

• *Use an oil or lotion:* You will have a luxurious, more sensuous experience. This lubricates your touch, eliminating the friction from your hand on your lover's skin. Select a massage oil or lotion that appeals to both of you. Pick something that feels good and smells good. Avoid heavy oils or anything with alcohol in it. Light vegetable or nut oils are good. Best oils for your skin: avocado, almond, apricot or peach kernel, soy, sunflower or olive. You can buy highly concentrated "essential oils" and add them as fragrance. Cedarwood, cinnamon, cloves, jasmine, neroli, patchouli, rose, sandalwood and ylang-ylang are all said to enhance sensuality. Make up small batches at a time. For every ounce of carrier oil, add up to five drops of essential oil. (Follow your noses!) Store the mixture in a cool, dark place to ensure freshness. Fragrant lotions are a great alternative if you don't like oils. Some professional masseuses even use baby powder instead of fluids.

• *Keep talk to a minimum:* Always tell your lover about anything that is painful or causes discomfort. Otherwise, the best time to talk during sensual LoveTouch sessions is *afterward!* If you are "taking turns," share your feelings between turns. Just apply the rules of LoveTalk: use specific rather than vague terms to describe your experience. Replace "great" and "wonderful" with descriptions like "flowing," "ticklish," "warm," "relaxing," "hard," "soothing" or "uncomfortable." Give lots of positive feedback, and be sure that any negative feedback you have is presented lovingly and constructively.

Preparing for Sensual LoveTouch Sessions

Here are eight more tips to ensure sessions of Sensual LoveTouch are everything you dream they will be.

1. Alternate roles.

2. Transition into a sensual mood by showering, bathing, eating lightly, slow dancing or meditating together.

3. Pick a comfortable, private spot. (There's no end to possible locales — the jacuzzi, shower, the office after hours — be creative!)

4. You're likely to want a firmer surface than most beds. Many people prefer a softly carpeted floor covered by a sensuously textured bedspread or other covering. Or try a futon similarly draped.

5. If you are the recipient, for frontal caresses, you may wish to place a thin pillow under your knees and the small of the back. Or when lying on your stomach for a back massage, put the pillow just below your knees.

6. The environment needs to be comfortably warm, so that neither of you becomes chilled. (But not so hot you'll perspire!)

7. When using oil or lotion, keep towels handy. You will need them for rubbing down the receiver at the conclusion

of the session. They are also useful for wiping away excess or mopping up a spill.

8. Heighten the mood — bring in the other senses as well. Select slow, sensual music like soft jazz, classical, world or New Age. Smells are wonderful, too — scented lotions and massage oils, scented candles, incense, or the popular essential oils that are mixed with water and heated by an aroma lamp. Go for soft lighting: candles or colored light bulbs. Bring in taste. Experiment with chocolate, strawberries in thick syrup, whipcream, or liqueurs. Or try some of the edible body oils advertised in magazines.

SENSUAL LOVETOUCH EXERCISE I
"Sensuous Stroking"

For your first sensuous LoveTouch session, set aside up to
an hour. Begin slowly, and take turns. For the first half of
the session, one of you should be the giver and the other
the receiver. Then switch.

Sensuous stroking is the key to sensual LoveTouch.
Once you feel comfortable with sensuous stroking, you can
move on into more advanced exercises during later
sessions.

Keep in mind that sensual LoveTouch requires a light
touch — it is *caressing*, not massage. The pressure of
massage can actually numb the skin. Caressing is a special
kind of intimate sharing, communicating your desire to
give her or him pleasure. Light stroking produces a far
greater richness of sensation because it activates nerve
tissue, not muscle tissue.

Begin with practicing different types of strokes, from
long and slow to quick and fluttering. Make sure, though,
that you establish a flowing rhythm with your strokes and
round off each stroke before moving to another part of the
body or changing the stroke you're using.

As a giver, you'll find you need to change your
position from time to time so you won't become
uncomfortable. That's okay. But, make it a point to
maintain body contact throughout when you change
positions or replenish oil. (If you are using oil, simply turn
one hand over, palm up, continuing to touch your lover.
Use the other to pour oil into your palm.)

The sequence goes like this:

1. Have your lover lie face-down, nude or near-nude.
2. Pour warm oil or lotion into your hands.
3. Begin stroking your lover's back, lightly.
4. Practice sensuous stroking on your lover's back.
5. Experiment — try any or all of the following strokes
   — or feel free to be creative.
6. Remove your hands *slowly* at the end.

Fan strokes: Fan strokes are wonderful for initiating sensual LoveTouch because they are both relaxing and ideal for applying oil to your lover's back. With your hands side by side, keep your fingers close together, pointed in the direction you intend to stroke. Glide your hands over your lover's body, distributing the light pressure evenly. As you caress, keep spreading your hands outward fluidly in opposite directions in the shape of a fan.

Circular strokes: These feel particularly good on the back, thighs, and along the sides of the body. Use one or both hands to produce continuous, rounded strokes.

Milking strokes: Great when stroking from the sides of the body to the center of the back, especially the waist and the hips — or for the front of the body. Sit or recline on one side of the receiver. Reach across and place one hand just a little under the far side of the receiver. The giver pulls his or her hand forward from the chest to the center of the back. Then the hand is lifted off and the same stroke is repeated with the other hand. This stroke can be very sensual since it caresses the contours of the body.

Stretching strokes: These do wonders on the legs, the sides of the body, the back and the spine. Place your hands together on one part of your lover's body. Move them lightly in opposite directions, producing a slight stretching effect.

Raking strokes: Bend your fingers slightly so you're only using your fingertips. Or, if the receiver prefers, your fingernails. Begin with short strokes. Use both hands side-by-side or let them work independently. Create variety, suspense and anticipation by "raking" at different speeds.

Feather strokes: Possibly the most sensuous of all strokes. Imagine your fingertips as feathers. Let them glide over your lover's body, one hand following the other. Vary the speed and pressure — lingering at times, barely touching the surface at others.

SENSUAL LOVETOUCH EXERCISE II
"The Full Body Caress"

For a head-to-toe frontal caress, you may experiment with the same strokes as described in the previous exercise for the back caress. If you're a woman and receiving, decide and let your lover know in advance if you wish breasts — or any other area — included or excluded as part of the exercise.

1. Warm whichever oil you use in your hands before applying it to your lover's body. Apply a little at a time to the section of your lover's body that you are stroking.

2. Begin all sensuous LoveTouch exercises by placing your hands gently on your lover's body. Hold them there for a bit. This establishes contact and gives you both a chance to start relaxing.

3. Begin initial sessions involving full-body caressing with your lover's back. Our associations to being touched there are primarily positive: pats, hugs, slaps on the back. Most people find themselves relaxing more quickly when touched there.

4. Whether giving or receiving, you'll find it more relaxing to move from the back to the legs and arms. Then move on to the main body area. Don't forget the hands, feet, neck and head. Be sure to include both the inside and outside of the legs as well as the upper surface.

5. The giver should continue moving gradually up the receiver's body with smooth, fluid movements.

6. When you reach the top, have your lover turn over.

7. If you're a woman, don't overlook spending a bit of time caressing your lover's nipples as you stroke his

chest. If you're a man and your lover has given you permission to include her breasts, this is your chance to become aware of them in a way you never have before. Do not, however, spend an excessive amount of time on them, to the exclusion of other parts of her chest and stomach area. When stroking breasts, use upward movements only, and be sure to be gentle with them.

8. Include the genitals in passing. But don't spend inordinate time on them. Above all, *don't stroke your lover's genitals to evoke a sexual response.* Sensual LoveTouch, not sexual LoveTouch, is your goal at this time.

9. When you're ready to stop, hold your hands in one place on your lover's body for a few moments. Then gently lift them away.

Afterward, be sure to discuss your sensations with your lover.

Repeat this exercise as often as you like — at least as often as is necessary for both of you to feel thoroughly comfortable and enjoy it as an end in itself. Only after you've reached that level of sensual awakening should you begin to include sensual LoveTouch as a prelude to sexual activity.

SENSUAL LOVETOUCH EXERCISE III
"Caressing Hands, Feet & Face"

Once you have mastered the full-body caress, you may want to experiment with something a little different. Try the same techniques on your lover's hands, feet and even face. You may be astonished at how sensual touching those areas can be. In separate sessions, give and receive sensual LoveTouch to all three areas. Let the receiver pick which it is to be. For the face, allow about ten minutes. For hands or feet, allow about fifteen minutes each.

Hands: Select a position that is comfortable for you both. Many people like to sit facing one another. If you are the receiver, allow your hand to remain limp and passive throughout the session. If you're the giver, pick up one of your lover's hands and don't let go until you are ready to move on to the other. Use your entire hand, the back, palm, your fingers to explore your lover's hand. Lightly stroke with your thumb and forefinger, making gentle, circular motions. As the giver, notice everything about your lover's hand — its texture, its folds, its creases, its shape, its thickness in various parts. Notice each finger as well as the fingernails. Once you sense that you're both comfortable, close your eyes as you continue stroking. You'll find the experience more intense if you do. Whether giving or receiving, do your best to concentrate fully on the sensations in your hands and the feelings evoked by these sensations. As the giver, linger a bit after you're finished with each hand. Try holding your lover's hand, palm downward, between yours a few moments before putting it down and moving on to the other.

The foot caress: Begin by bathing your lover's feet. If you're going to take turns, you'll need six bath towels and enough soap, oil, lotion, or powder for both of you. Next, fill two buckets or small tubs with warm (not hot), softened water. (The addition of a softener provides a wonderful fragrance and sensuously enhances the texture of the water.) You'll use one bucket for washing and the other for rinsing. Gather all these supplies together in advance so you won't have to interrupt the session once you've begun.

Sit on a comfortable chair with the bucket for washing between your legs. Gently place one of your lover's feet into the tub of water. Slowly wash the foot with soap. Leave it in the water as you move on to the next foot, repeating the process. After you've given each foot an initial washing, place a towel over one of your thighs, lift the first foot from the water and place it on the towel. Re-lather the foot generously and then place it in the rinsing tub. Repeat this procedure with the second foot. Remove each foot from the rinse water and wrap each completely in a dry towel. Push the buckets of water aside, unwrap one of the feet and slowly and thoroughly dry it. Be sure you dry carefully between the toes. Do the same thing with the other foot. Oil or powder them both.

Place the heel of one foot on your thigh so that you can easily touch both the sole and upper surface. Cradle the foot between your hands for a few moments to warm it, and then begin stroking. Beginning with the lower leg area, use both hands to stroke downward onto the upper and lower surface of the foot to relax it. Then move from the base of the toes toward the ankle, making circular motions with your thumb. Repeat several times.

Try using the heels of your hands, or several fingers together. Stroke every toe over its entire length, using your thumb and finger, and run your little finger slowly between each toe. Pay particular attention to the pad on the bottom of the big toe.

Vary the speed of your stroking. If your lover can accept the touching without being ticklish, try light feathery strokes and use your fingernails as well as part of your caress. If your lover is ticklish anywhere, try using a slightly firmer touching in that area initially, and see if you can later return to it with a softer touch. After ten or fifteen minutes, conclude by cupping your lover's foot between your hands for a moment, then gently remove them. Proceed to caress your lover's other foot in the same manner. If you decide to switch roles, with the receiver becoming the giver and vice versa, take about five minutes to share your feelings and reactions before starting the second session.

If your feet are ticklish, you can try to overcome it by desensitizing your feet. Being ticklish there (or anywhere else), may be your psyche's defense against their potential as a source of enormous sensual pleasure. Being ticklish allows you to avoid being touched and inhibits sensations that might become sexual. To desensitize the soles of your feet, go barefoot as often as you can. Walk on a variety of surfaces: cool tile, hardwood floors, grass, carpeting, sand, concrete, fabrics. This will also be a form of sensual awareness for your feet. It may sound silly, but your feet are richly endowed with nerve endings which, when stimulated, can produce extraordinary levels of pleasure.

The face caress: Having your face caressed is surprisingly relaxing and arousing. If you're a man, don't worry about being clean shaven; actually, whiskers' varied textures provide added interest. If you're a woman, remove your makeup. If either of you wear contact lenses, it's best to remove them, too. Get into a comfortable position that provides access to your lover's face. Sit with back support and a pillow in your lap, while your lover stretches out and places her head on the pillow. Or stand behind your lover while she is seated in a chair. Close your eyes if you're receiving. But keep your eyes open if you're the giver, at least until you've become thoroughly familiar with your lover's face. Remember as you are giving to stay focused on your lover's face and on the sensations you experience as the giver. You can experiment with both your fingertips and the palms of your hands. If you want to use a lubricant, a lotion is preferable to an oil; however, many people dispense with this entirely for this part of the body — especially around the eyes.

Begin by cradling your lover's face for a moment between your hands. Then glide your hands slowly upward through the hair and over the scalp. Move to the forehead area. Using your thumbs or your fingers, stroke from the center of the forehead outward toward the temples. Repeat several times. As you move downward, stroke the eyebrows. Then, ever so delicately, the lids and eyelashes. Do that several times, too. (Be sure to keep any lubricant away from the eyes.) Pause for a bit with your fingertips gently resting on your lover's eyes. Next continue down the face to the nose and cheeks. Use your thumbs to stroke downward on the sides of the nose and then outward just under the cheekbones. Glide your fingers upward through the hair before returning your thumbs to the nose. Then use gentle, circular motions with your fingertips on the cheeks, or experiment with the palms of your hands. As you move toward the mouth, stroke the area above the lip for a bit and then trace around the edges of the lips with your fingertips, following her or his contours. Then caress the lips themselves. As you proceed to the chin, try feathery downward strokes while continuing to move upward along the jaw line. Then move to the neck, continuing to stroke upward toward the jaw line as well. Continue to your lover's ears, using your fingers and thumbs to explore all of them, but don't probe inside them. Use both your hands to carefully lift and turn the head, allowing it to now rest in the palm of one hand. Use your other hand to stroke the exposed side of your lover's neck. After a while, turn and rest the head in your other palm and caress the other side of the neck. Finally, run your fingers through your lover's hair. Then bring your hands to rest gently on the face for a minute before releasing them.

After affectionate and sensual LoveTouch have brought you closer and fired your physical feelings for each other, you will want to reap the passion you have sown by moving on to the final stage, sexual LoveTouch.

11

SEXUAL LOVETOUCH
"Sex begins in the kitchen"

"Without sexual LoveTouch there would be no lovemaking and without lovemaking the relationship would not survive." (Joy, 26)

"Sexual LoveTouch is an important expression in our relationship, but we believe it should follow sensual LoveTouch — sex begins in the kitchen." (Kevin, 28)

"Sexual LoveTouch is the culmination of the sensual expression that is shared throughout the day. Sexual LoveTouch allows all the built-up love and energy to explode into complete fulfillment of giving and receiving the depth of each other's love." (Elizabeth, 39)

"Why is sexual LoveTouch important to my relationship? Because to me it is another form of telling my lover how much I love her. As well as making her feel good." (Andrew, 33)

"Sexual LoveTouch is important because it offers a unique kind of pleasure, pleasure that can both be given and received. It's also important because it is part of making love, and so is both an expression and experience of intimacy." (Sylvia, 48)

Affectionate and sensual touch deepen intimacy, bring us closer and arouse our passions. They make us hungry for the final step — touching each other sexually as a prelude to lovemaking.

Sexual LoveTouch includes touching each other in the most erogenous of all zones — between the legs. There's a fine line between sensual LoveTouch and sexual LoveTouch. Sexual LoveTouch has an aim: to bring about the physiological changes involved in arousal: increases in heart rate, blood pressure, respiration and muscle tension, and vasodilation of blood vessels in the genital region. In short, to turn you on!

Direct tactile stimulation of the genitals invariably becomes a part of sexual LoveTouch, while that region may or may not be a part of sensual LoveTouch. Sexual LoveTouch may or may not culminate in orgasm, but frequently does.

But don't make the mistake of skipping affectionate and sensual LoveTouch and jumping right to sexual LoveTouch. Moving into sexual LoveTouch without affectionate touching or a significant "dose" of affectionate lovetalk is a recipe for a disappointing sexual encounter.

In the preceding chapters, you've learned the vital importance of both affectionate and sensual LoveTouch. It's the expression of affection that establishes receptivity to even the possibility of sexual LoveTouch. And now that you have experienced the profound effect of sensual LoveTouch on spirit and body, you can fully understand how it prepares you to dissolve into sublime sexual LoveTouch.

Rule of thumb: If there has been little or no sensual and affectionate touching, you're not ready for sexy touching!

The Power of Passion

Never underestimate the power of sexual LoveTouch. It carries a very significant meaning for most people. At the most fundamental level, as one commentator wrote, it is a *"vehicle* for pleasure, self-discovery, attachment, and self-esteem."

Sex alone, even good sex, cannot make a sex-cessful relationship. But when sexual LoveTouch is at its best, it creates a sublime experience of connection that establishes a very special intimacy, a deep bond, between you and your lover.

Sexual LoveTouch is also the precursor of that vital element so many crave in a relationship: *passion.*

Dr. Robert Sternberg of Yale University has developed a "triangular" theory of love in which passion plays a crucial role. He believes that three key qualities come together in satisfying, long-lasting relationships, like the three sides of a triangle: *Passion, intimacy* and *commitment.* Thus, when passion is absent or minimal, you're missing up to a full one-third of the vital ingredients needed for a healthy sexual relationship.

It's loss of passion, the vital spark that keeps lovers interested in each other, that most people blame for break-ups, affairs and divorce. Without passion, a relationship limps along in a weakened, deadened state — continuously vulnerable to dissolution.

One common myth in our culture is that passion and sex are most important at the *beginning* of your relationship. Granted, the extreme highs that often characterize a romantic relationship are likely to fade over time. But don't discount the importance of a certain amount of sexual passion to the long-term health of your relationship.

"Passion and sex increase rather than decrease in importance over the first few years of a relationship," Dr.

Sternberg concludes in *The Triangle of Love*, "and decrease in importance somewhat over the very long term... As habituation sets in... the couple's ability to sustain some spark of passion and an interesting sex life becomes more and not less important."

Why is passion so important? After all, it's only the physical aspect of a relationship. Shouldn't we outgrow it? No, passion is the emotional charge that keeps lovers attracted. Passion motivates us to be close to each other and to want to communicate. When passion is missing, communication and closeness inevitably follow, leaving an emotional void in their wake.

What does sexual LoveTouch have to do with passion? Caressing your lover in that all-vital spot is both the cause and the result of passion. Sexual LoveTouch can even offer a profound encounter with your very being.

Although people vary in the degree to which passion is important in their lives, it's clear that a lack of sexual LoveTouch puts relationships at risk.

Relax — It's Not a Contest!

The English language, with its term "make love *to* someone," encourages the myth that you're supposed to "give" your lover sexual ecstasy, or "give" your lover an orgasm. (Romance languages more appropriately speak of "making love *with* someone.") Performance-oriented thought — such as "I wonder if I can make her come this way," or "He must be getting tired; I'm taking so long" — get in the way. They distract you from focusing on your sensations. The greatest gift you can give your partner is being lost in uninhibited enjoyment of the sexual pleasure being created between you.

Sexual LoveTouch Turn-offs & Turn-ons

Throughout youth and adolescence, society (parents, teachers, other adults, media...) tells us not to touch someone else sexually. Is it any wonder, when we finally enter into a long-term intimate relationship, that so many of us are not completely comfortable with touching or being touched sexually? Consider the baggage that gets in the way of what should be a pleasurable experience leading to physical bonding: social and religious prohibitions; poor body image; lack of self-esteem; inability to communicate effectively.

Another, and often overlooked, problem is that what's "sauce for the goose" is often not sauce for the gander. Sometimes your lover's characteristic way of touching you sexually may not be satisfying for you. Worse, it might be an actual turn-off.

When inhibitions prevent you from telling your lover this, sexual touching can grow to feel like an ordeal. You can begin looking for reasons to avoid it — perhaps going directly to intercourse. But without sexual LoveTouch you will soon find the passion has leaked out of your relationship. This is all too common a problem, and one with devastating consequences for the depth and longevity of your relationship.

Here are some typical turn-offs, as described by couples I surveyed:

Sexual LoveTouch that begins too abruptly: "My lover has been offended a few times if I touch him sexually to begin with. We both like to touch affectionately first." *(Ellie, 24)* "Sometimes my husband just expects me to drop everything and roll in the hay. He hasn't even bothered to hug me or ask me how my day went — nothing to show interest or make me feel connected." *(Tanya, 33)*

Sexual LoveTouch that is mechanical: "I hate it when his sexual LoveTouch feels mechanical — so many tweaks here and so many there, like it's rote." *(Carolyn,29)*

Sexual LoveTouch that is tentative: "My girlfriend is so tentative when she touches me sexually; it sure doesn't make me feel very wanted." *(Danie, 21l)*

Sexual LoveTouch that bypasses sensual LoveTouch and is narrowly focused: "Sexual LoveTouch is a turn-off when my husband goes directly for my breasts or thighs and ignores the rest of my body." *(Linda, 27)* "My lover is just absolutely obsessed with my breasts. I'm glad he likes them, but I need to be touched other places as well to get really turned on. And sometimes it makes me feel like I'm no more than a pair of tits, even though I know he loves me." *(Tara, 34)*

Sexual LoveTouch that is not reciprocated: "My wife just lies there sometimes when we're making love. I hate it when she's so passive; it feels like she's just accommodating me." *(Oscar, 42)*

Sexual LoveTouch that is too rough or too gentle: "My breasts are very sensitive, and sometimes my husband is just too rough with them, even though I tell him I need for him to be gentle." *(Margaret, 26)* "I don't like it much when my girlfriend sort of 'pets' my penis but won't take it firmly in her hand and stroke me." *(Terrell, 24)*

SEXUAL LOVETOUCH EXERCISE I
"Creating Anticipation, Yearning & Desire"

Enhance sexual LoveTouch with anticipation and ensure your lover's continuing desire during sex. Keeping the spark alive means creating a sense of yearning and anticipation before and during sexual activity.

One of the best ways to produce that sense of longing is to *slow down*. When you slow down your movements, it gives you a chance to mentally anticipate the next wave of pleasure, highlighting the classic adage that the brain is your most important sex organ.

Slowing down also makes for better sex. Nerve endings can "numb out" when over-stimulated by intense, rapid movement. Not surprisingly, the message of *How to Satisfy a Woman Every Time and Have Her Begging for More* was s-l-o-w d-o-w-n.

The following exercise will help you slow down, while heightening your lover's anticipation of your touch and bringing her to exquisite levels of sensory awareness and pleasure.

1. Take off your clothing and lie down somewhere comfortable with your lover.

2. Ask your lover to try to anticipate where you are going touch him or her next as you do the exercise.

3. Begin by holding your hands just above your lover's skin for a minute or two. Hold them close enough to allow your lover to sense the heat generated by your hands onto the skin.

4. Place your hands down gently on the same spot.

5. Lift them up again and pick a near-by area. Again, hold your hands above it for a minute before placing them on your lover.

6. Repeat until you've covered many different areas on your lover's body. *Here's a hint:* You're not restricted to just your hands. Feel free to place other parts of your body above your lover.

Now, take this technique one step further.

7. Rest your hands lightly on your on your lover's body for a while.

8. Tell your lover you are about to remove your hands. Ask him to try and hold on to the memory of your touch.

9. Lift your hands v-e-r-y slowly.

10. Give your lover a chance to really savor the sensation by waiting a bit before you place your hands down again.

With practice, your lover may not realize that you are no longer in contact for up to a minute or two after the hands are lifted!

SEXUAL LOVETOUCH EXERCISE II
"The Genital Caress"

You'll really fire each other's blood with this variant of the full body caress that culminates in genital touching. But before you begin, here's a sure-fire trick for heightening the pleasure sexual LoveTouch can bring to you and your lover: *Keep your attention focused on your own sensations.* It's just as important here as it is during sensual LoveTouch, but you may find it even more difficult.

(Make sure your hands are clean and your fingernails are smooth for this exercise).

For a particularly delicious experience, spend fifteen minutes giving your lover a back caress, then have him/her turn over for a front caress. This time, after caressing the torso, legs, arms, face and feet, for at least ten minutes, slowly — and gently — begin to include the genital area.

Put some water-based lubricant in the palm of one hand, then warm your lover's genitals by holding your other hand still over him or her for a bit. Beginning with your lubricated hand, slowly begin stroking your lover's genitals, alternating your hands.

If your lover is a woman, continue with slow, gentle, alternating strokes of your lover's vulva, exploring different areas. Try stroking and gently squeezing each of her outer lips, using your thumb on one side of a lip and your index finger on the other. Gently caress her inner lips, stroking especially on their inner surface. Let the intensity of her responses guide you in what she likes best, and take your time before you move to the clitoris. Add more lubricant as needed and stroke the perineal area at the lower end of her lips, stopping short of her anal opening. Lovingly caress her inner thighs. Using your thumb and index finger again, *lightly* pull a few pubic hairs at a time on her pubic mons (fleshy mound) area and outer lips. After a while, using your middle finger for extra delicacy, go back to her inner lips and travel up to her clitoris. Most women prefer to have it stimulated through the clitoral hood, rather than on the exposed clitoral glans itself. Using one or two fingers over the clitoral area, circle awhile slowly in one direction, then the other. Then, using more of your hand — your palm, the heel of your hand or all of your fingers — apply light to moderate pressure and make circular movements.

Many women also love vibrating movements. (Be sure you still have lots of lubricant before beginning this.) Begin with slow, up-and-down movements of your fingers over the clitoral area and gradually increase to a moderate speed. Keep your vibrating movements continuous and slowly travel down her lips, letting your middle finger slip between her two inner lips while your other fingers rest on the outer ones. Bring your hand and fingers slowly to a rest. With your middle finger still between her inner lips, begin using side-to-side vibrating motions for variation.

Now begin using one hand to caress her vagina internally. Let your thumb, with the pad facing the toward the clitoris, or "high noon" position of your lover's vaginal "clock," gradually enter. Press upward with your thumb while the fingers of that hand rest on her pubic mons area. Let your other hand rest gently on her lower abdomen. Don't stroke her vaginal wall yet. Instead, create pressure from your thumb by gently rocking back and forth about an inch. After a bit, release the pressure and move to the one o'clock position and repeat the rocking motion. Continue this rocking exploration with your thumb at each "hour of the clock" until you reach about six or seven o'clock. Then, switching to your index finger will make it easier to continue through the remaining "hours" and back to twelve o'clock.

Finish this exercise by simultaneously stroking your lover's "favorite time zone" (ask her for feedback!) with a "come-here" movement and gentle stimulation of her clitoral area. Slowly bring your hands to a rest before removing them and snuggling up with your lover. But maybe she has other ideas in mind...

If your lover is a man, after caressing other parts of his body and after you've placed lubricant or massage oil in the palm of one hand, assume a comfortable position before beginning genital stroking. You will probably want to be on his right side if you're right handed. Remind him to remain perfectly passive and to resist the temptation to touch you or actively move about. Although it's best to approach this genital caressing exercise without orgasm or ejaculation as a goal, it may happen. If so, let your hands rest gently on your lover before stopping. It's also best, for exploration purposes, not to follow this exercise with intercourse unless you specifically agreed to that beforehand.

Experiment with a variety of slow, erotic strokes. Don't be concerned about erection. The various genital caresses you try will feel wonderful to your lover, with or without an erection. Generously lubricate your lover's genital area, using upward, alternating hand strokes on his scrotum and penis. If your lover is uncircumcised, gently pull down the foreskin with your left hand to expose the head of the penis. Then encircle the body of the penis with your left hand and begin stroking slowly, up and down. With the fingers of your right hand, use a twisting motion to stroke the head of the penis. Do this as if you were slowly and erotically — and very gently! — juicing an orange on a hand juicer. Then, with the palm of your right hand, try making rapid circles over the tip of the penis. Try different pressures and discover what he likes best. Watch his face and eyes — listen for moans and sighs!

For another wonderful sensation, grip your lover's penis closer to the head with one hand while you use the thumb or a fingertip of your other hand to caress the frenulum (the inverted "V" spot on the underside where his foreskin was, or is attached). This is an extremely "hot" spot for many men. Then stroke lengthwise down the center on the underside of his penis, another common "hot" area. (Look and listen for more signs of pleasure!) Try rolling the penis between the palms of your hands, varying your pressure and speed (keep adding lubricant or oil!).

For a terrific variation on up-and-down stroking of the penis, try this idea suggested by Dr. Ray Stubbs in his *Erotic Massage: The Touch of Love*. Called the "Countdown," use lots of oil or lubricant and alternate your hands to make ten downward strokes on the penis and then ten upward strokes. Proceed to make nine downward strokes and nine upward strokes — ending with one down and one up. For added erotic sensation, syncopate your rhythm by pausing a moment after every two strokes (1-2—3-4—5-6). If your lover is highly aroused, you can try stimulating the base of his penis, in the perineum, behind the scrotal sac and before the anal opening. Use one hand to stroke up and down. With your other hand parallel to the penis, form a flat, paddle-like shape with two or three fingers. Make "paddle" strokes in the perineal area as you continue stroking the penis. Also try applying pressure with no movement of your paddle. (Be sure to get feedback from your lover about how this feels.) Continue stroking your lover's genital area in whatever ways appeal to you, and go with the flow. If you've previously agreed not to culminate in lovemaking, let your hands rest quietly on his genitals before you slowly and gently remove them.

SEXUAL LOVETOUCH EXERCISE III
"Showing Your Lover What You Like"

Want to evoke even greater passion? *Show* each other what
turns you on the most. Even couples who have been
together for years find deep-grained inhibitions (e.g.,
about touching ourselves sexually while others watch)
keep them from explicitly demonstrating how they like to
have their genitals caressed. But there's no time like the
present! You and your lover can guide each other by
demonstration.

Select a position that's comfortable for both of you; a
classic is for you both to be seated with your legs
outstretched, for example on a bed or a sofa, or on the floor
with your backs against a wall or other support. Whichever
one of you is to receive genital stimulation sits between the
legs of the other, with your back leaning against your
lover's chest. If you'd prefer to receive stimulation while
lying on your back, however, you may instead use that
position.

There are two ways to proceed here; you may try
either or both: One way is to *place your hands on your lover's
hands and guide them* in the ways that feel especially
arousing to you. Begin stimulating yourself as you would
if you were alone, and verbally indicate to your lover both
where and how you are touching yourself that feels good
to you.

The second approach is to *stimulate yourself with your
lover's hands resting on yours,* so your lover can learn in that
way what you like the best. Be sure you verbally
communicate what you like as one or the other of you is
stimulating your genitals.

Let your lover know in advance which of these
approaches you'd like to try initially, and do not feel
pressured to carry the stimulation to orgasm. If you are so
motivated, that's great, and if not, that's a wonderful
experience, too.

Touching each other sexually is the most intimate form of LoveTouch. Having become comfortable with it, BodyLove and LoveTouch, it's time to explore the ultimate love skill — the one that puts the fun in communication, sex and intimacy — LovePlay.

Love Skill Four:
LovePlay

12

SEX-CESSFUL LOVEPLAY
"Playful sex is so much fun!"

"The value of being playful sexually lies in the freedom and closeness it brings into the relationship. By gradually being able to open up more with my lover in a playful way, we become more open in terms of sex and other forms of communication." (John, 31)

"Sex isn't dull anymore, and it seems the more we play around in bed, the easier we can talk out of bed." (Isobel, 41)

"Playful sex is so much fun! Most important, it keeps the passion alive in an otherwise steady and predictable relationship."
(William, 29)

"Sexual play breaks the ice with my lover if we're both under stress and can't seem to find a way to begin to communicate again. Once we both start to laugh, everything else seems so unimportant."
(Leroy, 37)

Nothing averts stagnation and monotony — and keeps the spark alive in your lovelife — like sexual creativity and play! LovePlay is what this book has been leading up to. It is the spice that keeps couples interested in each other erotically and evokes the fondest, most exciting memories of amorous adventures.

These delicious moments allow you to really cut loose and have a fun sex life! Sexual creativity and playfulness are the final secrets to sex-cessful relationships. Though they're closely linked, the two are different.

Sexual *playfulness* is the spontaneous, often silly, things you and your lover do together. Think of sexual *creativity* as the wonderful, non-routine things that require advance planning. Sexual creativity and sexual play each make a special contribution to an exciting sex life for you and your lover.

In this chapter, we will look at the importance of LovePlay, give you the opportunity to determine whether there's a healthy supply in your lovelife, and get you started with a great suggestion hundreds of couples have used to add spark, excitement and fun to their lovemaking sessions. The next three chapters will lead step-by-step through the three forms of LovePlay — creative, oral and very daring LovePlay — helping you to expand your sexual limits and repertoire.

LovePlay: The Key to a Healthy Sexual Diet

The demands of work and children make it easy for human beings, as creatures of habit, to fall into their ruts. Faced with these competing demands and feeling exhausted, it's natural to fall into the "good old regular way" trap. Especially when you don't seem to have the time or energy for anything else.

Also, many people feel ambivalent — even guilty — about trying something sexually playful, new, or outrageous. Most of us have been conditioned to believe that "meaningful" sex must be "serious." Reinforcing this is the cultural message that play is something frivolous, irresponsible, and not for grown-ups.

Shaking off this kind of cultural baggage can be hard. But you've already broken through a lot of barriers in developing your LoveTalk, BodyLove and LoveTouch skills. You've learned how to overcome your worries about turning off your lover or yourself when you try new things. You'll need a similarly open mind as you venture into the new sexual territory of erotic creativity and play.

And, of course, most of us were only exposed to the "meat and potatoes" approach to lovemaking. We were never exposed to the wide variety of potentially exotic sexual "flavors." In fact, the parallels between a healthy, satisfying diet and a healthy, satisfying lovelife are many. Good eating and good sex both require *variety!*

As with sex, you may have a quick-but-healthy meal because you are pressed for time and want something simple but nourishing. Or maybe you have the leisure and desire for a truly sensuous experience and wish for fine dining. If you're not feeling too well, you may enjoy the soothing sensations of chicken soup. On other occasions, you grab greasy, fast food because it's easy or just because you have a hankering for it. And sometimes you get very daring and try new and exotic flavors from foreign lands.

If your diet is healthy and satisfying, you follow nutritional guidelines, avoid harmful extremes, and choose from a wide variety of foods. Within those limits, your selections reflect your mood and what appeals to you.

So it goes with sexual pleasure. Even though you may have a "favorite," sticking with "one flavor" (even if it's chocolate!), can get boring. Embracing a wide variety of sexual settings and activities — in keeping with your various sexual moods — makes for a wonderfully delicious and appetizing lovelife!

LovePlay also gives you more realistic expectations. You won't expect all of your sexual encounters to be profoundly meaningful or fulfilling in the same way. And you won't fall into the futile trap of feeling disappointment when sexual experiences aren't all the gourmet, "feast" type.

Being sexually creative and playful is also a wonderful way for you and your lover to express your erotic attraction and caring for each other. When you engage in LovePlay:

You show *trust* in your lover

You allow yourself to be *open* and vulnerable

You are *concerned* with your lover's pleasure as well as your own

You *communicate* intimately with your lover

You put *time and energy* into your sex life

• *Trust:* "The more I am able to be creative and playful, the more I trust my lover. I have to love the person to engage in certain activities with him. I would not share such things with just anyone." *(Dagmar, 24)*

• *Openness:* "When I am sexually playful, it is a sign of how comfortable I am with my husband. It is a sign I trust the relationship enough to make myself vulnerable. It also says I accept and love him no matter how goofy things can get in bed." *(Marcy, 28)* "I have learned that I can be myself, being creative without any restrictions. Sexual play involves trust, being open and communicative, being vulnerable." *(Bob, 24)*

• *Concern:* "Being sexually creative shows I will take time out to please her and think about her feelings." *(Hugh, 27)* "Being playful and creative is something I do out of love because I take interest in my boyfriend's pleasure as well as my own." *(Ali, 26)*

• *Communication:* "I believe being sexually creative and playful expresses acceptance of my lover. For me, it takes time to grow close enough to be able to 'let go' and become creative." *(Brooks, 22)* "It shows I am open to things because I love my lover. It means that I want him to be satisfied, along with myself. It also helps increase intimacy." *(Emily, 21)*

• *Time:* "People make their relationships too serious, and after a while the fun and excitement run out. So you must work on being creative and fun." *(Meg, 19)* "Being sexually creative and playful shows that I am willing to take the time and effort to make our sex interesting and enjoyable." *(George, 44)* "Sexual creativity and playfulness takes time, effort and planning. He knows I would not bother to be creative and playful if there were no love and caring involved." *(Florence, 54)*

Becoming more sexually creative and playful involves both letting your creative juices flow and moving beyond your inhibitions. In creative LovePlay you will learn to spice up your sex life with fun, creative new activities. In oral LovePlay you'll learn to remove the stifling inhibitions that get in the way of giving and receiving this most exquisite of erotic pleasures. Finally, in daring LovePlay you will discover how to expand your sexual boundaries by sampling pleasures some call "naughty."

The "Royal Treatment"

If you're looking for the ideal jumping off place for your adventure into LovePlay, try a technique I call the "Royal Treatment." Most of the couples I have worked with have reported great results! The basic idea is that one of you is elected "Royalty" for the evening and the other is the serving man or woman who must arrange lavish indulgences, cater to every whim, and literally give your lover the Royal Treatment.

Lovers who've tried this very special form of LovePlay only speak of its pleasures and delights: "We have done it for years. It is a wonderful idea! It gives you the freedom to take all you can take and then give all you can give... It's very special, brings you closer; it allows you to understand each other's sexual needs." *(Susan, 32)* "Having done this frequently in my last relationship, I can say it is a positive and exciting experience. I also must say that it is not only a wonderful experience for the 'king' or 'queen' but also for the 'servant'." *(Leslie, 27)* "My lover and I already incorporate what we call 'spoil time.' We alternate special days when one lover is pampered, receives more attention and decides how or when we will make love. We both find this experience gratifying and intimate." *(June, 29)*

Some couples even like to plan Royal Treatment nights on a regular basis, especially if they have busy schedules and feel overworked. Such evenings prevent the erosion of intimacy and passion that often occurs when "more important" things get put first — before lovemaking and your relationship. There is no more creatively fun way to show your lover how much he or she is cherished, appreciated, and not taken for granted.

Here is the way some people would like things to go on Royal Treatment Day (or Night): "I sit down in the backyard, my wife is cooking, bringing me what I want. When I want specific things involving sex, she does it without me asking." *(Ben, 39)* "He'd put on an apron, serve me and do anything I wanted him to. If I wanted any specific sexual choice he would be willing. Massages, showers, anything." *(Dianna, 29)* "I would like to be 'Sultan' instead of 'King.' She would be my favorite. I would enjoy a good bath and rub down with oil, with some harem music of course." *(Tito, 26)*

Here's how some people planned to show their love when giving the Royal Treatment: "I would start by making my wife feel like the most important person in the world. I would cook her favorite meal. Then I would serve it to her naked. I would then give her a full body sensual massage. Then I would prepare a warm bath full of oils and herbs. I'd finish the evening by doing anything sexually that she would want." *(Karl, 37)* "I would begin by slipping an extra bag of vitamins into his briefcase with a note saying, 'You'd better take these; you're going to need them tonight!' which would get his curiosity going all day. Then I would leave a sexually explicit message on his voice mail at work. I would have no 'one-on-one' conversation with him until he comes home. I would have all the lights turned off and candles going up the staircase with Barry White playing in the background. A glass of champagne would be waiting for him at the top of the stairs. On the floor would be a trail of my clothes leading to the bedroom... the door of the bedroom would be closed, when he opened the door the room is filled with candles. I would be on the bed naked except for my beautiful sequined and feathered mask around my eyes and a beautiful boa draped around me and, of course, don't forget every man's fantasy... stiletto heels. I would have his favorites... caviar, brie, crackers, Kama Sutra honey dust powder, massage oil. The works... I would then tell him to rub my tummy and make a wish!!! Whatever he wants... his wish is my desire. Then he can just lie back and enjoy!" *(Helena, 34)* "I would orchestrate a 'king' night by having a secluded hotel suite where no interruptions could interfere — no telephone, no visitors. I would have satin sheets on the bed and a rose on his pillow. I would also have his favorite champagne on ice. I would have lots of his favorite foods and snacks on hand. I would fill the room with scented candles and turn the lights down low. I would play his favorite slow songs on an automatically changing C.D. player. I would run him a hot bubble bath and wash his entire body. Then, I would towel dry him and give him a hot oil massage. I would then feed him pasta with my fingers and allow him to indulge in the other foods on the menu. I would then proceed to sing to him while looking into his eyes with lots of emotion. I would finally tease him until I knew he was about to explode. Finally, I would act like his love slave and make passionate love to him all night long." *(Michelle, 31)* "I would choose a fabulous room in a hotel in Malibu or Laguna Beach. I have a crown that I would set on his head and tell him that he is the boss. I would make sure that we had an ocean view and would be able to hear the waves hit the shore. The room would also have to be equipped with a jacuzzi. We would first order room service so that he could have his favorite meal. In addition to whatever he ordered, I would have strawberries and cream for later. After dinner, I would run his bath water. We would take a bath together and turn on the jacuzzi. I would suck his toes and feed him the strawberries and cream. After the bath, I would give him a full body massage. I would then tie him to the bed and do whatever he asked me to do. I would wear a French maid's outfit with crotchless panties and let him have his way." *(Ronette, 38)* "My Queen would be taken by chariot to a hotel, have a hot bath and flowers awaiting. Room service with her favorite food. Dessert to be eaten off her. All of her favorite sexual pleasures done for her." *(Clark, 38)* "I would start a Queen Night by getting a limo and going down to Newport Beach to eat at our favorite restaurant. On the way home I'd have the limo drive through the hills so we can watch the sunset. Once home I'd give her an oil massage on her whole body, beginning with her back." *(Nigel, 40)*

SEX-CESSFUL LOVEPLAY EXERCISE I
''Do You Have a Healthy Loveplay Diet?''

It's time to assess the amount of creative fun in your lovelife. Ideally, each of you should take this self-quiz—then use your LoveTalk skills to discuss your results. Place a check mark by the phrase that seems to reflect your own feelings most strongly:

1. How much LovePlay do you think there is in your relationship at present?

      A. ☐ A little? B. ☐ A moderate amount? C. ☐ A lot?

2. How much routine would you say there is in your lovelife?

      A. ☐ Too much? B. ☐ A moderate amount?
      C. ☐ Too little?

3. How do you feel about the possibility of trying erotically creative and playful things with your lover?

      A. ☐ Reluctant? B. ☐ Moderately willing?
      C. ☐ Eager anticipation?

4. How easy is it for you to think of creative erotic ideas?
      A. ☐ Not very? B. ☐ Moderately? C. ☐ Very easy?

5. How difficult is it for you to suggest a new sexual activity?

      A. ☐ Very? B. ☐ Moderately? C. ☐ Easy?

6. How often do you engage in fun, creative LovePlay?
      A. ☐ Less than once a month? B. ☐ Once a month?
      C. ☐ Several times each month?

Three or more "A"s in your score suggests your relationship needs a prescription for a large dose of LovePlay to stay healthy. Mostly "B"s indicates there is some LovePlay, but a healthier dose might add some missing spice. If you checked at least four "C"s, you are among the lucky couples who already have a healthy, playful lovelife.

SEX-CESSFUL LOVEPLAY EXERCISE II
"Giving Your Lover 'The Royal Treatment'
for an Evening"

Set aside a complete evening for this exercise. If there are children, send them to a relative. Turn off all phones, pagers, etc.

Decide which of you will receive Royal Treatment and which will be the servant for the evening.

The person selected as servant fulfills whatever requests the designated royalty desires — throughout the course of the evening.

Alternatively, plan an evening around an activity you know your lover would like (a movie, sporting event, wild sex, theater, etc.) — even if it's one you don't normally enjoy. Or make it an event you both would thoroughly enjoy.

With the need for increased play in your lovelife clearly in mind, and a hint of what it can bring from trying the Royal Treatment exercise, the next step is increasing the fun in your lovelife with creative LovePlay.

13

CREATIVE LOVEPLAY
"Fun things that feel good"

"I think of creative sex as the subtle little fun things that feel good. These things are done just to show love, not necessarily to have it lead to sex. Rubbing his head while kissing his forehead. Kissing his ears. Tickling his toes or stomach. Holding his hand and rubbing his fingers while we're watching TV." (Vicki, 38)

"I've often wanted to try more role playing with sex. This would be done verbally and also acted out. Maybe as far as dressing-up."
(Amber, 22)

"For me creative sex means grabbing the massager out of the drawer, offering to massage her back, then applying it gently to her vulva area. She instantly smiled and laughed." (Andre, 32)

It's time to begin having fun with sex! Be creative and let your imagination run wild with this most bountiful of all Love Skills! Draw from all the basic Love Skills to sex-cessfully add lots of delicious variety and zing to your sex life with creative LovePlay.

By now you have likely gained confidence in your ability to stretch your sexual limits and are open to trying something a bit more erotically imaginative and adventuresome. These might be sexual activities that you'd like to do once, just because you'd like to be able to say you've done them! Other times, they're adventures that initially feel as if you're "pushing the envelope," but later become an integral part of your LovePlay.

The trick to creative LovePlay is to balance your desire to try something new with your need to feel sexually comfortable with what you're doing. As sex therapist Marty Klein, author of *Ask Me Anything*, puts it: "Eroticism lives at the intersection of the need to feel safe and the desire to risk." Use LoveTalk to jointly pick and choose from among the many LovePlay ideas below. Never do anything that makes you feel uncomfortable and try out only those that appeal to both of you. See "Resources for Lovers," page 217.

Tip: Keep a positive attitude. Congratulate yourself for being brave enough and trusting enough to venture into new sexual territory. The results can be delicious! And remember the old adage, "nothing ventured; nothing gained."

Creative LovePlay: Getting Started

Creative and playful sexual experiences pull you out of sexual ruts by providing variety and spice to your sex life. Here are over two dozen LovePlay suggestions other couples found helped add zest, romance and eroticism to their relationship. Because it's normal to have many different ideas about what's sexy and what's daring, some of the ideas may even seem tame to you, others may have already been part of your lovelife for a long time!

• *Playing with senses.* There's something daring and exciting about giving up one of your senses during sexual activity. Being blindfolded, for example, by making you more vulnerable, can boost your psychological excitement and heighten the sensations of touching, hearing, smelling and tasting.

Tip: For an intriguing twist on voluntarily "giving up" a sense, consider a "nonverbal evening," during which you spend the entire evening in silence — eating, dancing, playing! (Moans and sighs are O.K.!)

• *Playing with pictures.* Having your own, personal "boudoir" photo shoot can add fun, entertainment and an instant turn-on to your love life. Polaroids have never been more fun! Or, videotape yourselves making love and then play it back.

Tip: Be sure that *both* of you are *genuinely* open to this idea before proceeding. And, as certain media exposés have demonstrated, it's probably your best bet to destroy (erase) the "evidence" immediately after use.

• *Playing with sexy messages.* Phone messages, personal notes and racy greeting cards offer endless possibilities for spicing up your love life. All offer opportunities for injecting surprise and anticipation. Stuff suggestive, playful notes or cards in your lover's briefcase or suitcase, or mail them to her office marked *"personal."* (Be sure to find out if the mailroom staff respects such notations!) Leave messages on a private phone machine or on private voice mail. Pagers offer interesting possibilities, too. (One woman's lover used to call her pager and enter 69-69-69 whenever he felt like letting her know he was thinking of her!)

For more daring, try phone sex with your lover. Phone sex is great when you and your lover have to be separated, when you don't live together or — if you have more than one line in the house — simply for wicked variety. Remember to use your sexiest, sultriest voice. For a wonderful look at more exciting possibilities, rent the movie, *The Truth about Cats and Dogs*.

Tip: If you're at a loss for what to say or write, read a passage from an erotic story or a witty line from a greeting card.

• *Playing with time.* Do you and your lover usually make love at the same time of day or night? There's nothing like a change of schedule to perk things up. Whether it's "afternoon delight," a predawn encounter, or an entire Sunday in bed, try a new time at least a few times each month — more when you can!

Tip: Try squeezing a sexual rendezvous into an extended lunch hour on a work day. Or take a mini-vacation. There's nothing like a getaway to rejuvenate passion. It offers a change of scenery with no distractions and a chance for one-on-one intimacy and romance.

• *Playing with attire.* Sex appeal BodyLove (Chapter 7) introduced you to the charms of dressing up for each other in sexy, alluring clothes. It's also fun to make love partially clothed — or while wearing costumes for an evening. Or wear something sexy and let your lover only caress you — but go no further that evening.

Tip: For extra spice, go out on the town in your sexy garb. Or add the element of surprise by meeting your lover publicly in nothing but a coat — or go to the movies or dinner with no underwear. Make your lover temptingly aware of your "condition," either visually or by guiding his or her hands.

• *Playing with stripping.* Many people — both male and female — report they'd like to do striptease for their lovers.

Secretly plan it as a surprise, or just let it happen spontaneously some time when you're in a daring mood.

Tip: Although stripping is usually associated with women, male strippers are increasingly popular. If you're a truly uninhibited man, you'll perform for your lover, too. The results might prove surprising.

• *Playing with paints:* Let the artist in you escape and boldly use your lover's body as your canvas while indulging in bodypainting. You'll both find it sensuous, erotic, and fun. Choose from moist grease paints used for stage, old lipsticks and other make-up items, or body paints sold for that purpose. (Some of these itch after they dry — make sure they guarantee "non-itching." Whatever you use, be certain it's *water soluble!*) If your lover is willing, you might even carefully use scissors to "design" her genital area while you're at it.

Tip: It's safest to do this on top of a sheet or blanket you're not worried about staining. You might want to take pictures of your artwork before sudsing it off together in the shower!

• *Playing with roles.* Role-playing adds variety to your lovemaking while providing a subtle way to explore desires that might be awkward under other circumstances. There's no end to possibilities: from the proverbial patient in need of a "very private" examination by the doctor, to flight attendant/passenger, priest/nun, French maid/master, homemaker/repairman, Anthony and Cleopatra — and whatever are your own fantasies and inventions. Remember, the focus is on daring, erotic role-play. As one male said: "I'd love to try role playing, like my girlfriend dressing up in a leather-studded bathing suit with extravagant make-up. Like something you'd see in a *Mad Max* movie. She could take me and just do anything she pleased with me except whips and things that would hurt."

Tip: Role-playing is only fun if you *both* like the idea and get pleasure from it. If you or your lover feel shy or inhibited, approach this very cautiously. If role-playing is easy for you, you might videotape your "show" for added excitement.

• *Playing with location.* Holding your amorous interludes in different places can heat up even the most basic sex. Your own home offers many erotically-charged possibilities for LovePlay — from the shower to the dining room table, the backyard, balcony or hammock. You can even jazz up the setting by pushing two sofas together to create a "lovenest." Other couples have had their most memorable LovePlay experiences on secluded beaches, elevators, roofs, airplanes, parks, in grassy fields, restaurant bathroom stalls, under restaurant tables, parked in a parking lot, on a hike deep into the woods — and dozens of others. The possibilities are as unlimited as the number of potential locations.

Elevator: "I'd like to try a mall elevator (glass or not), standing up while its moving and then coming to a stop in the middle of the elevator shaft. Actually in an elevator like the one at the Bonaventure Hotel in Los Angeles would be nice." *(Christopher, 27)*

On a beach: "I'd like to make love on a beach with everything perfect — bring candles and light them around us."*(Margit, 31)* "I would like to go to the beach one night and have sex in several different places like the guard tower, the water, the sand, the bathroom, and the parking lot, or some other public places like that." *(Larry, 30)*

Public places: "I'd like to try sex in a less-than-private place, a park or a car in the daylight." *(Ivan, 25)*

Striptease: "I'd love to do a striptease/lap dance for my husband." (Marissa, 29)

In a car: "I'd like to try having sex with my boyfriend in a limousine. *(Sheree, 18)*

On a roof: "I'd like to have sex on top of a roof during a full moon." *(Amanda, 35)*

Tip: Sometimes "external" experiences happen spontaneously; other times, they're better off planned. The thrill of "possibly" being caught is a better bet than "probably" being caught! *Be cautious, not foolish.* In either case, make sure you have something you can pull over you for an instant "cover-up." And do pay attention to the legal risks. One lover's "fantasy" may be a law enforcement official's "indecent exposure."

• *Playing with surprise:* A sexual surprise, however simple, can deepen intimacy or inject fun into an otherwise routine evening. It could be flowers, a room full of balloons that say "I love you," dressing up sexy, or kissing your lover from head to toe.

Tip: Shaking up your partner's expectations this way can energize the lovemaking that follows and pull you out of the same old "rut."

• *Playing with possibilities:* There is no end to the possibilities for LovePlay. Here are some that others have found rewarding. Put your own original twist on any of them.

Flowers: "I purchased ten dozen roses and put petals throughout the bedroom as well as filled a bath full of petals." *(Wolfgang, 47)*

Strip-tease: "I made him dinner and then stripped. This was a surprise for him because I'm really shy about my body." *(Pam, 29)*

Nude greeting: "I bought a variety of candles and a romantic tape, cooked a romantic dinner, and met him at the door with nothing on." *(Crystal, 31)*

Gift wrap: "I greeted him at the door with aluminum foil all over me on Valentine's Day and told him to unwrap me — I was his Valentine's gift." *(Marianne, 32)*

Body-painting: We once planned a surprise together where we painted each other using body paints. I am an artist, so using body paint really thrilled me." (Ian, 37)

Wrestling: "Loving play includes rolling around/wrestling on the floor together; kissing and not expecting it to always lead to sex." *(Ron, 26)*

Joking about faults: "We like joking about our physical faults and loving the other for them, and touching each other's 'weak spot.' " *(Norma, 51)*

Creative kissing: "When we are in bed together at night sometimes, I'll kiss him from the top of his neck down to his bottom along the spine. It does not always have to lead to intercourse but the slightest touch in one spot can be arousing." *(Mary, 38)*

Teasing and flirting in public: "Sexy LovePlay could be going out to dinner and teasing my husband by licking my lips slowly and eating my food in a very sexy way and telling him that 'I will tear you up when we get home.' " *(Hester, 38)*

Dancing nude: "Sexy Loveplay could be dancing together naked." *(Darcy, 20)*

Shaved pubis: "I shaved my pubic hair, then initiated sex. When he took my underwear off, was he surprised!" *(Jillian, 31)*

Planning Sexual Encounters

Of course you've had terrific spontaneous loving play with your lover. But wonderful, memorable sexual experiences, especially loving, creative ones, are often the result of planning ahead. If you've been reluctant to plan sex in the past, it's time to throw away the "spontaneity myth." Spontaneity is not the only legitimate way to approach sex. In fact, there are lots of advantages to planning sex. Knowing in advance when you and your lover are going to be sexual gives you more time to do all the things that make you feel confident, sexy, and eager:

- *Bathe and groom.* Many people feel at their sexiest when they are freshly bathed, showered, shampooed, shaved, aftershaved, perfumed, manicured, moisturized and the rest.
- *Dress in a sexy, alluring way.* Putting on something you know your lover would find sexy is always guaranteed to add stimulation to your lovemaking.
- *Eliminate distractions.* If you are at home, let the answering machine do its job, turn off the TV and pager, make plans for the kids and get rid of any other possible sources of distractions.
- *Go away for a night or two.* Getting away for an evening or weekend is an ideal way to say your love life is special to the two of you — while keeping intrusions or distractions to a minimum.
- *Set aside more time.* If you and your lover have hectic schedules, not planning sex often translates into little or no lovemaking at all. It means you can pick the best time for sex (not at "bedtime," when you're exhausted).
- *Create a sexy or romantic atmosphere.* Planning sex at home or in a secluded motel allows you to set the stage and provide just the atmosphere and mood you want. If it's romantic, you can arrange the flowers, set up the candles, select just the right CDs. If it's sexy, you might wear something that turns on your lover, purchase a special massage oil, or rent an erotic film.
- *Introduce fresh, creative elements.* Planning ahead allows you to introduce new sexual ideas into your LovePlay that you have both agreed would be interesting to try.
- *Get your sexual imagination started.* If you have difficulty dreaming up hot new sexual activities, planning ahead gives you time to fantasize and get your creative juices flowing.
- *Demonstrate your love and appreciation through your creative energy.* If you are the exclusive "planner" for the

evening, the thoughtfulness, creativity and care in pleasing your lover sexually is a powerful sign of your love and appreciation.

• *Build anticipation to intensify your sexual experience.* Advance planning sparks anticipation that acts as a powerful aphrodisiac, according to psychotherapist Jack Morin. His studies found anticipation an "erotic intensifier," playing a key role in triggering peak erotic experiences. As one woman put it: "I fantasized over and over about what I was going to do to him and how I thought he would react to me. It allowed me to come up with the best possible way to knock his socks off — plus I was totally aroused and willing to go anywhere with him to make his fantasy come true for both of us."

Tip: Let your mood determine your special loving sex encounter. Whether you plan a simple surprise, a special evening at home, or a complete get-away weekend, don't fall into the trap of thinking that cost reflects the specialness of the occasion.

CREATIVE LOVEPLAY EXERCISE
"The LovePlay Suggestion Box"

Now that your head is buzzing with great suggestions for fun, creative LovePlay, you may have trouble deciding where to start. The following exercise will get you started — and help keep you going.

1. First, create a "LovePlay Suggestion Box."

2. Sit down together. Write down on slips of paper any of the above ideas for LovePlay that appeal to you both.

3. Fold up each suggestion and put it in your Suggestion Box.

4. Write down other ideas and stuff them in the box whenever they occur to you. Keep it stocked with fresh suggestions.

5. Any time you want to try something different and playful, simply fish out a slip of paper and do whatever it says. (If you draw a mystery activity that doesn't appeal to you at the time, toss it back in and select another that does!)

6. Dip into your LovePlay Suggestion Box often. The more you use it, the more fun you'll have! You'll also feel more comfortable and hone your LovePlay skills.

Now that you have tried so many delightful, sexy and fun ways of playing with sex, you should be ready to give what many people consider the most intensely pleasurable form of LovePlay — oral LovePlay.

14

ORAL LOVEPLAY
"...Such a tremendous feeling of closeness"

"I love both giving and receiving it. I can't think of anything I don't like about it. It gives such a tremendous feeling of closeness."

(Hiromi, 34)

"I love giving oral sex! It's my favorite thing in the world. It's sensual and erotic. It's a turn-on for me to turn-on the other person."

(Perry, 28)

"My lover is healthy and clean, so I haven't any dislikes about it. I love the smell, the taste, everything. I also enjoy receiving oral sex. It's great! I like the warmth of it, the intensity." (Wade, 27)

"I love receiving Oral LovePlay from my husband. It's the best pleasure I've ever had. I cannot climax with intercourse only. However, with Oral LovePlay I can." (Susan, 32)

"I love oral sex. I feel that the mouth and hands are such communicators of love. They are for me the truest and simplest way to know someone physically. To know every part of one's body by taste and touch and to be able to give and receive pleasure."

(Clara, 38)

The special pleasures of oral LovePlay are legend, offering you and your lover a very special way to deepen your sense of physical and emotional intimacy. The mouth and tongue are great resources for creative stimulation. Because the tongue is softer than fingers and saliva provides a natural lubricant, tongue movements provide a deliciously different — and often more intense and pleasurable — kind of stimulation than the sensations experienced during intercourse. Not surprisingly, for many people — especially women — oral sex is the easiest way to reach orgasm.

(Of course, there is another kind of "oral" LovePlay: Turning your lover on verbally by whispering sweet nothings and sexy somethings. If you skipped it, you'll find guidelines and suggestions for arousing you both in the sexy LoveTalk section of this book.)

Oral LovePlay — the physical type — has big payoffs for both giver and receiver. It's yet another wonderful way to be creative sexually. Oral LovePlay also reduces the pressure of having to have intercourse during every erotic encounter. In becoming intimately familiar with this very special part of your lover's body, you heighten your sense of intimacy and connection. Many people experience it as their ultimate "love gift," as Dr. Alex Comfort calls it in the *Joy of Sex*.

So for many, oral LovePlay is a good place to start expanding boundaries. Because it's so common today, the concern that you're not "normal" is uncommon. Because you probably already have some experience with it, oral LovePlay can be among the easiest pleasures to further explore.

Uncomfortable? You're Not Alone!

Oral LovePlay, though a common practice, continues to pose difficulties for many lovers. Though many enjoy it thoroughly, others are quite willing to give or receive it, but have hang ups of one kind or another about reciprocating.

Moreover, oral LovePlay is one of the most common sources of sexual frustration: one lover likes it; the other finds the idea distasteful. Negative reactions include:

Concern about taste and smell

Being unhappy with the "hard work"

Feeling awkward or inexperienced

Feeling suffocated when giving cunnilingus, or gagging during fellatio

Feeling emotionally or physically vulnerable when receiving oral LovePlay

Taste and smell: "I don't really like performing oral sex because I don't like the taste or the smell, and I don't like getting hairs in my mouth." *(Catherine, 37)*

Hard work: "One thing I don't like about giving oral sex is that it's tiring." *(Darla, 33)*

Feeling awkward: "I think I'm uncomfortable because I really don't know what to do." *(Stuart, 34)*

Suffocating: "I don't like it when my lover forces my head into her." *(Eli, 23)*

Choking: "One man I was with in the past was so big I always choked." *(Nikki, 28)*

Vulnerability: "I've never enjoyed getting oral sex on first encounters. It's a matter of giving up something of myself and I must trust to do that." *(Morris, 47)*

Some responses are even more negative. There are lovers who perform it — but only reluctantly as a "concession" to their partners. Some surround it with restrictions: she may be willing to perform fellatio, but only if he avoids ejaculating in her mouth; he may practice cunnilingus — but not after she has had her period, or after he has ejaculated in her vagina.

If you are older lovers, you may have grown up believing oral LovePlay is somehow "unnatural" or "perverted." That's one of the biggest, most harmful and persistent myths. Although many feel (unnecessarily) uncomfortable, heterosexual oral LovePlay is very widely practiced and desired.

The Gift of Giving, The Gift of Receiving

With experience, practice, and patience anyone can become comfortable and adept at heating up their lovemaking with oral sex — as giver and receiver. Honest communicating and creative problem-solving can help — apply your vertical and horizontal LoveTalk skills. It involves a combination of listening to feedback, experience and willingness to learn.

Paying attention: "I've become skilled by paying attention to my lover's reactions and by talking to him and asking questions. I use all the senses and tune in to my lover, listening to his breathing sounds, watching his facial expressions, feeling his muscles tense and relax."

Experience: "Practice, practice, practice!"

Feedback: "Sometimes I'll ask my lover what feels good. For example, I'll ask him if he likes it when I stroke his penis while giving him fellatio, or if he likes it when I rub the inside of his thigh while performing oral sex." *(Madeline, 37)* "I don't mind asking what feels good. Being told or shown is O.K., too (no sensitive ego in that department)." *(Dave, 47)*

Willingness to learn: "The first thing I did was ask him to get me a magazine with pictures so that I could see what I was supposed to be doing; then I just paid a lot of attention to what he moaned the loudest at." *(Kristy, 26)* "It was a combination of watching videos and experimentation." *(Jay, 33)*

Trial and error: "Trial and error basically sums up how I have gone about becoming skilled at giving oral LovePlay. I do what comes naturally and if she doesn't like it, she'll tell me. If she does like it, then I hear no complaints and remember what I did for another time." *(Stefano, 29)*

Media: "It was a combination of experimentation and watching pornos." *(Jeff, 33)*

Tips for Better Oral LovePlay

• *Tips for performing fellatio:* If you're concerned about gagging or choking, you can control how much of the penis you take into your mouth. Either use your hand to guide it toward your cheeks — or hold back the depth of penetration by circling your hand or hands around the base.

You might have difficulty with the idea of your lover ejaculating in your mouth. If so, ask him to signal in advance when he is about to ejaculate. *If there is any reason to be concerned about the possibility of disease, refuse to perform oral LovePlay unless he wears a latex condom.*

If — or when — you are willing to try receiving your lover's semen in your mouth, have him first ejaculate outside your mouth. Then place a little of the fluid on your finger. Feel it, smell it — put a few drops on the tip of your tongue to taste it. Repeat this several times, until you feel comfortable with him ejaculating directly into your mouth. (After accepting his semen, you can transfer it into a glass, into Kleenex, or simply swallow it.)

As an initial foray into fellatio, ask your lover to remain perfectly passive and to refrain from thrusting whatsoever. The more control you have, the more you're likely to enjoy your role as the giver. Also, be sure that the penis remains pointed upward; bending it down too far during oral stimulation can be painful.

• *Tips for performing cunnilingus:* One common concern about performing cunnilingus is the heavy, musky vaginal scent. For some it's a turn-on — but for some it's a turn-off.

If you have a problem with this, you can almost completely eliminate odor by waiting until your lover is freshly bathed.

Over time, you're likely to find yourself becoming attracted by her natural, vaginal scent. That's because a woman's intimate fragrance contains pheromones (chemical substances with sexual attractant power). Foul odors, especially after bathing, are a sign of something physically wrong — not a woman's natural, healthy scent.

Another problem for some is taste. Again, this should be reduced by bathing. If one soap leaves a bitter aftertaste, try another, such as a honey-scented one. Avoid the flavored douches, syrups, or other sweetened lotions and oils sold at "erotic boutiques" — they can trigger infection. Stick to natural, water-based lubricants such as K-Y Jelly™ or Ortho's Personal Lubricant™.

If you're worried about feeling suffocated, ask your lover *not* to press your head into her. If you're worried because you are a beginner and aren't certain what to do, ask your lover what she likes. If you have trouble finding a comfortable position, try pillows or other props, or positions such as sitting or kneeling.

Remember that most women prefer to have the clitoris stimulated through its hood; the tip (glans) of the clitoris is often too sensitive for direct stimulation. After a while, the clitoris may retract under the hood, seeming to disappear after a while, causing you to suddenly "lose" it. This is perfectly normal and signals she's highly aroused. You may find that pressing your palm upward on your lover's lower abdomen will enable you to "retrieve" the clitoris.

But don't make the mistake of focusing exclusively on the clitoris. Be sure to use both your tongue and hands to explore her entire vulval area.

• *Tips for receiving cunnilingus.* If you're concerned about vaginal odor, bathe just before sexual activity. You can make it more fun by showering with your lover. But keep in mind that a natural, healthy scent can also be very arousing. Believe your lover if he tells you he prefers the fresh, natural fragrance that you have a few hours after bathing.

Don't try to mask your scent by using sweetened or scented products inside or near your vagina. These products can cause a yeast infection. Consult with your physician if you notice any unusual or unpleasant odor — it often signals an infection.

If you're the type who worries that your lover doesn't "get anything" out of giving you oral pleasure, ask what he likes about it. And *believe* what you are told! You'll probably be as surprised as the woman who said, "He told me that he loves me and wants to bring me pleasure just as I do him!"

Tips for receiving fellatio. Although most people love receiving oral LovePlay, there are some common concerns. Some fear feeling vulnerable. Others worry about being injured if the LovePlay becomes too aggressive.

If you're more accustomed to being "the active lover," you may experience initial difficulty at being the one to lie back and passively enjoy intense pleasure. The secret is to be willing to give up control, as one man noted: "I love fellatio — it's a mix of pleasure and vulnerability, and of trusting my lover."

See Glossary, page 207 for help with terminology.

LOVEPLAY EXPANDING REPERTOIRE EXERCISE
"Becoming Skilled at Oral Loveplay"

Feeling skilled as a lover is certainly an important part of feeling sexually comfortable and confident. Becoming a skilled giver of oral LovePlay takes a little practice, a willingness to try using your mouth and tongue in a variety of ways, and good communication with your lover.

1. Decide in advance of your practice session if you each want to experience giving and receiving, or if you'll stick to "one-way."

2. Allow yourself plenty of time. It's a good idea not to begin immediately with oral stimulation of the genitals. Start out with lots of kissing and other forms of foreplay first — that helps you and your lover to relax and to anticipate.

3. Gradually let your mouth make its way to your lover's genitals. Once there, you can lick, suck and nibble (careful with the teeth!).

4. Experiment with slow strokes, fast strokes, light pressure, heavy pressure. Explore the entire genital region, asking your lover to let you know what feels particularly good.

5. Don't forget to use your hands in creative ways (there are no rules against letting your fingers "internally explore" at the same time!).

When both of you feel comfortable with the idea, the following chapter offers suggestions and guidelines for safely expanding your sexual horizons with daring LovePlay.

15

DARING LOVEPLAY
"...Why not try if it's not going to be harmful?"

"I've always been sexually conservative, and I'd like to throw that out the window one time and just be a naughty girl."   (Julie, 37)

"For me, really expanding my sexual limits would mean trying things that when I think of them offhand, I think, 'Oh god, that is disgusting!' But at the same time, I wonder about it. If you have a comfortable and trusting relationship, why not try if it's not going to be harmful?"   (Hassan, 37)

"Expanding my repertoire means that I finally indulge with my partner in some activity that I've never done but wanted to do."
(Les, 39)

"I think of being experimental, releasing inhibitions. To me this would be with people who are extremely close. I also view this as a very positive sexual experience."   (Rich, 33)

(Caution: You may find some material in this chapter to be offensive. Proceed with caution. Many lovers have found the ideas and practices in this chapter stimulating and satisfying; however, if you feel your own comfort zone being challenged too closely, by all means skip to the concluding chapter. Return only when — and if — LoveTalk leads you both to agree you would like to reconsider the material.)

Having discovered how to set fire to your lovemaking with the fun of creative and oral LovePlay, it's time to consider taking a step beyond your normal sexual boundaries, expanding your sexual limits. With daring LovePlay you will explore some of the so-called "naughty" and "forbidden" avenues of sexual expression open to you and your lover. These are the activities you've been curious about but feel reluctant to try — sharing sex fantasies, watching erotic videos together, using sex "toys," and others.

It's perfectly understandable if you feel more than a bit uncomfortable about trying some of these activities. Whenever you expand old limits of any kind, sexual or otherwise, it's normal to feel a bit of apprehension. After all, you're stepping beyond old, familiar boundaries into unknown territory.

But you're reading this book because you have a vision and a goal: you honestly want to make your loving sexual relationship all it can be. You are also someone who believes enough in yourself and your lover to be able to envision this possibility. Through Love Skills you are learning that this means trying new things and participating in the evolution of your own erotic relationship.

There will be inevitable bouts of discomfort and awkwardness as you experiment with the new, develop new attitudes and even feel new feelings. If you're sometimes tempted to fall back into sexual routine or reject something different, that's perfectly normal, too.

But you also have learned by now that working through those feelings of doubt can be well worth it. It's when you transcend your usual limits to reach a goal that you feel the most alive and vital. While stretching limits can be scary, the results can be exhilarating.

Going beyond your current sexual limits into the territory of "forbidden" and "taboo" erotic behaviors can sound frightening at first. You're likely to experience such fears as: "Am I normal?" "What will my lover think if I suggest trying out this activity?" Or "What if I'm completely turned-off by it?"

Fortunately, there are fun ways to get up the nerve to successfully cross your previous erotic boundaries. Most, if not all, boundaries you and your lover decide to cross together will turn out well as long as you don't just blindly jump into the deep end of the pool — way beyond your personal comfort zone.

Crossing erotic boundaries can even result in truly memorable, peak sexual experiences, according to research by psychotherapist Jack Morin. He has reported that thirty-seven percent of couples shared peak sexual experiences while engaging in "prohibited" amorous behavior. Morin describes the positive impact on "adult eroticism" of "violational behaviors and fantasies." He calls this aphrodisiac effect of violating prohibitions the "naughtiness factor."

Daring LovePlay has many other potential benefits. It can:
- *Add zest and passion* to your sex life
- *Help you discover and explore* new forms of
     sexual activity
- *Boost your sexual confidence*
- *Increase your sense of closeness* with your lover

> *- Reduce the sense of deprivation* that arises when
>   one of you likes something the other is
>   reluctant to try
> *- Help you feel sexually alive and growing* — not
>   stagnating
> *- Open you to new things* in general, making
>   you less intimidated by the unknown.

Guidelines for Daring LovePlay

The suggestions below will help you develop the
courage to try out daring, limit-challenging sexual activities.
These are "hot tips," based on solid psychological principles
and the practical experience of thousands of lovers I've
interviewed and surveyed. They will show you and your
lover how to safely, gradually increase the range of sexual
activities you enjoy to include all the naughty, forbidden
things you've always dreamed of — but didn't know how to
comfortably put into practice.

• *Establish ground rules.* Trust is a basic requirement
when trying anything sexually new. You can reduce any
concerns you might have through vertical LoveTalk by
agreeing to choose jointly which activities to try first. It's
important to agree in advance not to judge each other (or
yourself!) as you share ideas, even if some feel
unconventional or "kinky." Agree that each of you will have
uncontested "veto power" over any sexual activity that
bothers you — and *at any point* during it. Mutual consent is
an absolute necessity here. Establish any other ground rules
that either of you feels would be helpful.

• *Use "baby steps."* Follow a "baby step" approach that
eases you into new sexual recreations a bit at a time on several
successive occasions — rather than diving into them head
first.

• *Establish your comfort zone.* When some new activity that interests your lover makes you feel uncomfortable, take a few minutes to discuss what conditions might make it easier for you to try. In fact, for each new activity you're interested in use vertical LoveTalk to establish your comfort zone first. Here's a sampling of what others have found helpful to them:

Discuss it in advance: "It would make it easier to try fellatio if my lover suggested it, or if I talked to him about it first." *(Carrie, 21)*

Increase privacy: "It would make it easier to play striptease if we had more time set aside. I would want us to have the house to ourselves." *(Tom, 38)*

Plan carefully: "I think it would be easier to try this new adventure if it was planned." *(John, 37)*

Pamper: "I'd need to help my lover to be more receptive by pampering her." *(Felipe, 25)*

Be willing and responsive: "It would make it easier to experiment by having a lover with the same curiosities who is also willing to try. He would have to be sensitive and stop if it becomes uncomfortable or just not right." *(Janice, 24)*

Fantasize about it together: "It would be helpful to talk about the idea casually, to the point where it becomes more of a fantasy than just something to talk about. Maybe then we would be able to work up enough courage to try it." *(Bart, 29)*

• *Identify the rewards.* Consider all the possible personal and erotic rewards the new sexual activity could bring to your lovelife. For one thing, there's the excitement of novelty and variety. For another, there are the possible sexual benefits. If you're a woman who doesn't experience orgasm during intercourse easily and you've never tried using your own hands to simultaneously stimulate your genital area during intercourse — experimenting with masturbation may be the key that unlocks your climax. Finally, it may satisfy a sexual "itch" or yearning that has been driving you crazy or frustrating you for years.

• *Discuss what has stopped you in the past.* When you find yourself reluctant to engage in a particular new activity, use vertical LoveTalk to explore the factors that make you feel that way. For example, one woman's list included: "Having the lights on: This is scary for me because it makes me so visible. I know my husband says it would be a big turn-on for him, but I just hate how my stomach looks."

• *Choose an official "stop" word and/or time limit.* It's important to agree to an official "stop" word. If either of you becomes too uncomfortable you can use it — and the other *must stop* what ever you are engaged in *immediately*. This provides a sense of control and can make it easier to partake in scary activities.

• *Share feedback.* After trying anything daring and new, discuss how each of you felt. If it was positive experience, share the news "horizontally" afterward. You can also explore any "adjustments" or different approaches you'd like to consider next time. If you experienced difficulties, save them for vertical LoveTalk. Avoid an immediate, horizontal feedback. You will be able to express yourself more clearly and your lover will be in a more receptive mood to hear it after you are out of bed.

Exploring New Erotic Territory

Daring LovePlay includes exploring new territory. Here are some ideas I've gathered from many sources. Some are more daring and adventurous than others; remember to let your comfort zone be the guide. Feel free to "mix and match" whatever elements hold special appeal to create your own unique daring LovePlay experiences. Once you and your lover have integrated a new activity into your love life, try another and another!

• *Sharing turn-on fantasies.* Sharing your sex fantasies with your lover can add fun and excitement to your sex life, be a real turn on — and bring the two of you closer together. Our erotic fantasies range from the romantic "we're on a desert island" to far-out things you'd never want to actually enact like "orgies" — both kinds are normal and rarely problematic. They are, after all, just fantasies — thoughts and daydreams that flit through our minds — not something that necessarily has substance.

For most people, telling their most intimate, secret and "naughty" sexual fantasies to their lover sounds scary — no matter how close or intimate they feel. Often they are afraid they'll make themselves vulnerable — shocking their lovers or turning them off. But more often, they become a turn on, an aphrodisiac that adds extra potency to your lovemaking. (And, as most of us know from personal experience, fantasies give a big boost to masturbation experiences — together or alone.) Sharing your fantasies frees you to introduce even the wildest notions into amorous encounters, without the risks of acting them out. They can:

Increase excitement and intensity: "Fantasies during sex can add to the excitement and intensity of the act. And it has increased our knowledge of each other's needs and desires." *(Charmayne, 27)*

Strengthen relationship: "Sharing fantasies has strengthened my relationship because I feel I have nothing to hide from my lover when she already knows my fantasies." *(Gilbert, 39)*

Keep monogamy from monotony: "Sharing fantasies with my lover has allowed me to feel that my sexuality is not limited just because we are exclusive." *(Wayne, 41)*

Build intimacy: "Sharing fantasies has made our relationship much more exciting because we act out our fantasies. It also makes us feel much closer than before, when we didn't share our fantasies." *(Janice, 34)*

Tip: Agree to each share a fantasy, and share them when you're the most comfortable. It doesn't matter when that is — just before love-making, during love-making, during the afterglow of love-making or when you're nowhere near the bedroom. It could be during a candle-lit dinner or on a stroll. Use LoveTalk to set down any ground rules either of you need. For instance, do either of you have a problem with (or would prefer) hearing a fantasy where your lover has sex with someone else — or with one that involves someone you actually know? Or, do either of you have an objection to (or would prefer!) fantasies your lover would actually like to act out? Best of all, start with your tamer fantasies first. Then work your way by mutual consent and exploration to the most daring!

• *Viewing erotic videos together.* Erotically themed videos come in many forms: from Hollywood movies like *Bull Durham*, to art films like *sex, lies & videotape*, soft "R" like *Exit To Eden*, and X-rated films like *Red Shoe Diaries*. All these, and many others, are currently available on video tape for rent or purchase and on the sex-oriented cable TV channels. (You'll find a list of titles to consider in the "Resources for Lovers" section at the end of this book.)

At first, the thought of watching erotic films is problematic for many people — and can become a source of contention between couples. We were raised to believe that visual representations of nude bodies — and especially of people making love — are "obscene," "pornographic," "dirty," "sinful" and worse. So if one or both of you experiences aversion at the thought of watching erotic material, you have a lot of company.

It can help to consider the difference between the *erotic*, which is a valuable part of your relationship, and the *pornographic.* Pornography can be seen as material that contains almost nothing but explicit shots of sexual acts — close-ups of the genitals as intercourse, oral sex or whatever is taking place. Erotica focuses primarily on an on-going, erotically charged tone through looks, words, filmy lingerie, discreetly lit shots of breasts, chests, buttocks, close-ups of hands touching legs, lips on a lover's eyes, a long shot of bodies twining together — but may or may not include explicit shots of genitalia and intercourse.

Of course, the judgment is largely in the eye of the beholder. "If you like it, it's erotic. If you don't, it's pornographic!" What's important, if you'd like to explore this avenue, is to use LoveTalk to select things that appeal to you both — and not just one of you.

One other important element in these films: *violence.* I certainly do not advocate activities that are demeaning or abusive to either partner. While "the eye" of every "beholder" will assess such material differently, I encourage you in your choices to place the emphasis on sexual eroticism, not abuse.

Tip: Literally thousands of possibilities exist at your local video store. If you feel uncomfortable renting erotica there, try out late-night movies on premium cable channels like HBO™, Showtime™, Cinemax™ and others. They frequently show "soft" erotica — and you can watch them cuddled up together in the comfort and convenience of your own bed.

• *Reading erotic stories to each other.* Find a piece of writing that arouses you and share it with your lover. After reading something you like to your lover, ask your lover to read the selection to you. Then let your lover choose a selection for each of you to read. Either way, read with your most sensuous, sultry voice.

Tip: If either of you has difficulty finding something suitable, go to a local bookstore and select something that personally turns you on. (Tip-within-a-tip: Try both small independent stores and huge chain "superstores." You may be surprised at the selection available.) Your choice might include emotional scenes where one character declares love for another, or it might be a scene of explicit sexuality from a romantic novel or erotic classic. Whatever it is — get it, take it home and read your selections to each other. (You'll find a list of racy volumes — available at most bookstores — in "Resources for Lovers" at the end of this book.)

• *Using erotic accessories:* Sex toys and accessories are readily available and if you've never used any before, they offer many opportunities for erotic fun and play. They come in a wide variety of types — since different people are aroused by different things and in different ways. Surveys show that among the most popular are vibrators, dildos, feathers, flavored massage lubricants, edible panties, restraint devices (bondage materials, ropes, chains, etc.), penis rings, clitoral and penis stimulators (mini-vibrators), anal inserts — to name only a few.

In major cities, you're likely to find well-maintained specialty stores for an adventurous outing. If there's no store in your area, or it's too embarrassing to go, there are several excellent catalog companies. (See "Resources for Lovers.")

Vibrators are the most popular, according to a survey by the Lawrence Research Group Advisory Board. This woman's comments show why: "I like to use a vibrator while straddling my husband. Most women who straddle a man get more clitoral stimulation, but that's not true for me. Since my husband enjoys me on top, a vibrator works great."

Tip: Explore the erotic possibilities of a vibrator together — or alone. Vibrators are famed for their ability to help a woman reach orgasm — particularly those who have difficulty doing so or obtaining sufficient stimulation from a penis alone. However, many men experience wonderful sensations when the tip of the vibrator is gently used around the rim of the penis head and especially on their frenulum (the inverted "V" area on the underneath side of the penis head).

But don't just restrict yourselves to the genital area — other areas of the body have sensuous and erotic possibilities, too. Experiment with the pleasurable effect of different speeds.

An erotic "accessory kit." Set aside a drawer or special spot in your bedroom (safe from children, if that's a consideration) for a sensuous "accessory kit." Stockpile erotic sex toys, erotic literature, massage oils, body paints, feathers and other accessories for an evening of pleasurable BodyLove. And take it along when you jaunt off together on vacations and getaways!

Tip: If you forget your "kit" on a trip, put on your "erotic lenses" and take a stroll down the aisles of a supermarket. You'll find a good selection of feather dusters, scented or votive candles, oils, lotions, cornstarch (for a massage on *their* sheets), whipped cream, chocolate sauce, honey, champagne. With a little imagination, you can substitute these — and other items — for your missing erotic accessory kit.

There are many other sexual activities, of course. Some of these "daring" activities are considered by some to emphasize sex rather than love, while other couples find engaging in them to deepen their own intimacy and emotional feeling for each other. There is not room to include every possibility here, but if you wish to consider them further in the context of enhancing your committed love relationship, other guides are available. Most such activities — e.g., anal sex, bondage and discipline (aka dominance and submission), and "threesomes" — are described in popular magazine articles on sex, XXX-rated films, and erotic literature.

DARING LOVEPLAY EXERCISE
''Expanding Your Erotic Boundaries''

The step-by-step exercise below will help you test the daring LovePlay waters safely, gradually and at your own speed. Keep in mind the guidelines from creative LovePlay (chapter 13) and make sure your comfort zone requirements have been met before you engage in any form of daring LovePlay for the first time.

1. Use vertical Lovetalk to select a daring LovePlay activity that you have never tried but would be willing to experiment with.

2. Set aside unpressured time.

3. Discuss any concerns either of you feels about trying the activity.

4. Determine how you might relieve or reduce those concerns.

5. Discuss the attractions it has and the pleasures you believe it might bring.

6. Reinforce your love, caring and commitment to each other.

7. Proceed at your own pace and comfort level.

Acquiring the four basic Love Skills — LoveTalk, BodyLove, LoveTouch, and LovePlay — gives you unlimited potential for enjoying all the erotic possibilities in a sexual relationship between two loving people. But, as with any skill, practice makes perfect. In the concluding chapter of this book, you'll find suggestions to help you keep your LoveSkills fresh, as well as how to get the most out of them.

Sex-cessful Love Skills for Life

I hope you're pleased with the benefits your Love Skills adventures have produced in your lovelife, and that they've brought you as much fun as I promised. I'll bet that practicing LoveTalk, BodyLove, LoveTouch and LovePlay have increased the communication, intimacy, fun and sexual pleasure in your life.

The end of a book often brings a sense of let down. "Is that all there is?" "Isn't she going to tell us how to...?" And the new adventure we began together a couple of hundred pages ago is about to end. But your newly energized love relationship is just beginning! Let the momentum of the fun you've had together inspire you to continue using and honing your skills, and having even more fun with them in the future!

In this final chapter, I'm going to offer you a few guidelines for extending your Love Skills throughout your erotic journey together.

• *Continue the "baby steps" approach.* As you've read this book, you've been gradually introduced to new ideas and exercises for heating up your lovemaking. Even though you might be feeling so confident you're tempted to break away from it, stick with this gradual approach awhile as you further develop your Love Skills. This tried-and-true method guarantees permanent results and success.

• *Have fun practicing your new found Love Skills.* To become an "artist" at lovemaking, you have to *use* your Love Skills! You can do this several ways. Repeat any of the exercises you particularly enjoyed or found especially helpful. Retake one or more of the self-assessment exercises to see how your answers have changed. Or try an exercise you feel comfortable with now but skipped over previously because it made you uncomfortable.

• *Periodically review a section.* It's perfectly normal not to assimilate everything the first time around (or, for that matter, the second!). Often, you'll find yourself picking up a helpful point that you missed before. Reviewing can also remind you of ideas or suggestions you liked but had forgotten.

• *Focus on the positive; don't strive for perfection.* Honing your Love Skills is *not* synonymous with achieving perfection. Resist any perfectionist tendencies you may have. You undermine the benefits when you allow yourself to become critical and judgmental of yourself or your lover. As is true of any other human activity, it's unrealistic to expect perfection of your Love Skills. On occasion you may even experience a "two-steps forward, one-step back," pattern. Simply focus on delighting in your *overall* forward progress. Stick to a positive mind set that focuses on the ways that your sex life is getting "better and better."

• *Continue your journey as co-creators.* Make Love Skills a joint adventure. Jointly evolve creative inspirations for extending your Love Skills. Maintain a mutual spirit of good will and respect for each other and your limits. Remember the power of affectionate LoveTouch to soothe and nourish yourself and your lover. Use vertical LoveTalk skills to resolve differences you might have about sexual preferences.

• *Embrace balance.* Maintaining balance in your lovelife reaps dividends. Balance keeps you from falling off the deep end. For example, one client, concerned that his use of masturbation to help him fall asleep was "abnormal," was assured that it was not, since this was neither his sole sexual outlet nor his unique masturbatory pattern. One couple raised the question of "planned" versus "spontaneous" sex, and learned that, for most people, a blend of both provides optimal balance — the "best of both worlds."

• *Maintain your integrity.* You cannot feel good about yourself or your sexual relationship in a profound, spiritual way unless you are true to your own values. Don't "sell your soul" in the apparent service of your sexual relationship. In other words, don't avoid ethical conflicts in your love life by selling your personal integrity out and doing something you don't want to do just for your lover's sake or because you feel diffident about discussing it. If you do, both you and your relationship are in deep trouble. Differences in values, needs, desires, and preferences can pose special dilemmas in your sexual relationship. For example:

You like sex in the morning; your lover likes sex in the evening.

You like the idea of planned sex discussed in LovePlay skills; your lover thinks it's contrived and only wants spontaneous sex.

You and your lover don't agree about how often you enjoy being sexual together.

You like lots of variety in your sexual activities; your lover is uncomfortable with it.

You and your lover have "conditions for good sex" that are at odds with each other (they may merely conflict, or one of you may have a very extensive list, while the other does not).

One of you may be totally turned off to sex.

One of you may want your lover to try sexy clothing and he or she may be reluctant to agree.

One of you may be requesting permission to step outside the primary relationship for sexual satisfaction, or may be suggesting that you "swing" with others, while the other finds these unacceptable suggestions.

The earlier mentioned items on this list are generally easier to negotiate than the latter. But with a little stick-to-itiveness and following the rules of LoveTalk, you will find you can work through the most difficult challenge to reach a solution satisfactory to both without either of you selling yourselves out.

The morning/evening debate, for instance, is often solved by using LoveTalk to communicate with your lover about your preference. Once you can get a good handle on the specifics, you can often creatively resolve the difficulty. For example, it may be the your primary objection of morning sex is that you always feel rushed to get to work afterward. If that's the case, and your lover really likes morning sex, you might agree that morning sex is restricted to weekends or days off, etc.

When you and your lover enjoy regular sexual activity, but the conflict is about the specific frequency of sex, LoveTalk may help you to resolve the issue. Don't just passively go along with something you don't like. Remember, the goal is not to have *more* sex; it's to have *more fulfilling* sex.

Each human being has unique desires, motives and conditions for sex. If you and your lover respect each other's individuality, applying your new and growing Love Skills — LoveTalk, BodyLove, LoveTouch and LovePlay — should enable you to resolve any sexual conflicts and to fulfill your erotic needs without compromising your integrity.

EXERCISE
"Savoring the Rewards of Love Skills"

It's natural to falter in any process, even something as sexy and fun as using your Love Skills. The exercise that follows will help keep you excited about having acquired them and motivated to continue the adventure. It asks you to focus on the many benefits you and your lover have gained from learning Love Skills. They might include better communication about sex, a healthier acceptance of the physical aspects of sexuality, the fiery response of sexual touch or the excitement of sexy clothing. It differs for each lover, of course. Simply put down your own.

1. Each of you should have a notepad or other method of making a list.

2. Separately, jot down as many of the positive changes brought to your lovelife by each of the four skills. You can use the sentence stems below to help get you started.

3. "Because of LoveTalk we/I now

_____."

4. "Because of BodyLove we/I now

_____."

5. "Because of LoveTouch we/I now

_____."

6. "Because of LovePlay we/I now

_____."

7. Now fill in this final one: "Because of Love Skills in general we/I now _____."

8. Share your responses with each other and use LoveTalk to decide where you'd like your Love Skills journey to take you next.

Love Skills Tips
for Anxious Moments

The *Love Skills* program has been designed to minimize feelings of discomfort. Nevertheless, you may find that some of the exercises or activities suggested create some anxiety in you or your lover. Using one or more of the following procedures will be very helpful in alleviating or eliminating discomfort.

BABY STEPS. Psychologists call this procedure "successive approximation." The idea is to approach the desired goal very gradually, taking only one small "baby step" at a time, thereby experiencing as little anxiety as possible along the way. With each small step you're a little closer to your goal, and you've remained calm as you've progressed. Here's an example:

In Affectionate Lovetouch Exercise III, page 113, you were encouraged to look at the list of ways your lover would like to see your affection expressed and to try a new way each week. "Baby steps" are best accomplished by first arranging, from easiest to most difficult for you to try, the items on your lover's request list. Then, week by week, progress from top to bottom through the list. (*Tip: Resist the temptation to please your lover by beginning with the item he or she said was the most important, if it's not the easiest for you to accomplish.*)

Similarly, to reduce feelings of discomfort when trying any of the *Love Skills* exercises or suggestions, consistently use this "baby step" approach of gradual progression from easier to more difficult. For maximum benefit, do any of the following relaxation exercises that appeals to you *before* taking each baby step.

RELAXATION EXERCISES. It's not possible, speaking physiologically, to be relaxed and anxious at the same time. So, if you can teach yourself to relax in the face of uncomfortable situations, you can overcome your anxious feelings and fears. The process — called "systematic desensitization" by psychologists — begins with learning to relax fully and completely. There are a number of approaches to choose from. Here are a few:

Deep muscle relaxation. The goal of this procedure, also known as *progressive relaxation*, is to bring about relaxation of your entire body by learning to distinguish between sensations of tension and deep relaxation. You can accomplish this by focusing your attention progressively on each of four major muscle groups in your body: 1) hands and arms; 2) face, neck and shoulder area; 3) chest, stomach and lower back; 4) buttocks, upper and lower legs and feet.

To begin, find a comfortable position and relax, either lying down or seated in a chair that provides head support. Next, scrunch up one muscle group and hold the tension for five to seven seconds. Then instantly release the tension, as if turning off a light switch, and let that area remain relaxed for twenty to thirty seconds. To heighten your state of relaxation, focus on the contrast between the sensations of relaxation and tension. You may also find it helpful to accompany your release of tension with a relaxing self-suggestion such as *"Feeling relaxed and calm"* or *"Letting go more and more."*

Repeat this procedure at least once, and several more times if that muscle group remains tense. Then move on to the next muscle group, repeating it at least once, and so on, until you have tensed and relaxed all four major muscle groups.

Note: Like all the *Love Skills* exercises and *Love Skills* tips, deep muscle relaxation occurs more readily with practice and repetition. If you do two fifteen minute sessions per day, you can expect significant gains in your ability to calm your body and feel relaxed in one to two weeks.

Breathing. Typically, when you are anxious, your breathing is shallow, often irregular or rapid, and through your chest (your chest expands and your shoulders may rise when you take in air). By contrast, natural, relaxed and unconstricted breathing is abdominal or diaphragmatic. Diaphragmatic breathing is one of the quickest and easiest ways to relax yourself.

Begin by lying down or sitting comfortably with arms and legs uncrossed and your eyes closed. Inhale deeply through your nose, letting your abdomen rise. Then pause before you exhale through your mouth, releasing a whooshing sound. Focus on the sound and sensations of your breathing, coming back to them if your mind wanders. You may wish to silently repeat a comforting word (for example, *calm* or *peace*) as you let your breathing get even slower and deeper. Continue for five to ten minutes, once or twice a day for several weeks.

The positive, relaxing effects of abdominal breathing are immediate. With months of daily practice, you're likely to experience more profound benefits.

IMAGERY. The mind is capable of "inventing" a situation so real that, for practical purposes, it might as well be happening. Although we vary as individuals in our ability to visualize, most of us can create powerful mental images and use them to bring about important life changes. As a tool for handling anxiety, imagery is as useful as any available to us. For example, athletes often practice visualization, repeatedly imaging themselves succeeding in games and matches. Speakers use imagery to prepare themselves to address large gatherings with ease. And you can use imagery to overcome your reluctance to do some of the uncomfortable exercises and activities in this book. It can help you think positively. Here's how it works:

1. *Get in a comfortable position, close your eyes and begin with one of the relaxation techniques above.*
2. *Pick a simple goal* (for example, a *Love Skills* exercise that evokes only a bit of discomfort when you think about doing it).
3. *Create a clear mental image or idea of your goal.* Imagine your goal as already existing as you want it to be. Evoke all of your senses — sight, touch, hearing, smell and taste — as you imagine it in as much detail as you can.
4. *Use short, positive statements.* Also called "affirmations," these are brief statements that help you focus on your goal in a positive, encouraging way. Always phrase them in the present, and avoid negative phrasing. Here are some examples that could be especially appropriate for *Love Skills* exercises (be sure to create phrases that are comfortable and effective *for you*):

I'm feeling relaxed and confident.
My lover's caressive touches feel incredibly wonderful and
  arousing.
My lover's body (or hair, chest, thighs) looks so beautiful.
I can smell the wonderful aroma of the scented candles.
I'm feeling really trusting... I'm letting go.

5. *Evoke your imagery often.* Initially, focusing on your imagery may be easiest while lying in bed, just before rising in the morning or retiring in the evening. You'll get the full benefits of imagery as you practice and are able to evoke it whenever and wherever you want.

Note: You may notice immediate results, or it may take several weeks of practice. As you achieve simpler goals, you can move to a slightly more difficult one.

SELF-VALIDATION AND SELF-SOOTHING. Although it's wonderful to receive encouragement and positive feedback from your lover, you're ultimately responsible for overcoming your fears, frustrations, disappointments and sorrows. To overcome anxieties or other negative emotions, psychologists encourage self-validation and self-soothing techniques. Here are a few:

Replacing distress-maintaining self-talk with self-soothing self-talk: Often, your discomfort about trying something new is triggered by negative self-talk, the inner statements you make to yourself that produce negative emotions such as fear, anger or anxiety. Because these statements are distorted, exaggerated distress-maintaining thoughts or beliefs, they are often referred to by psychologists as *automatic thoughts, irrational beliefs* or even *crooked thoughts.*

By whatever name, they share common features. First, they falsely create the impression that things happen to you to "make" you feel a certain way, rather than accurately reflecting how your *interpretation* of events produces your feelings. Second, these statements often include overgeneralized, perfectionistic, and absolutistic *shoulds, oughts, musts* and *can'ts, always* or *never,* or "awfulizing" phrases — phrases that make dire interpretations and predictions about your experience or the situation you are in.

Distorted, distress-maintaining self-talk such as *My lover couldn't possibly find me attractive* or *I'll never be able to use lovetalk during lovemaking* make it difficult for you to feel good about yourself, your lover, or your relationship and can interfere with feeling ready to try the various exercises and suggestions offered in the *Love Skills* program.

To begin replacing distress-maintaining self-talk with more accurate, self-soothing self-talk, you'll need some paper — better yet, consider using a notebook to start a "Self-Soothing Journal." Then carry out the following steps (adapted from Martha Davis, Elizabeth Eshelman and Matthew McKay, *The Relaxation and Stress Reduction Workbook*, [4th Ed.], Oakland, CA: New Harbinger, 1995):

1. Write down *the facts* regarding the situation and what is or was bothering you. Leave out your opinions, feelings, interpretations.

2. Write down *what you say to yourself* about the situation. Now's the time to include your assumptions, value judgments, beliefs, concerns and catastrophic predictions.

3. Write down *a brief description* of your emotional response. Use just a word or two, or a sentence at most (for example,*Very anxious*).

4. Write down *an active challenge* to the validity of your distress-maintaining self-talk listed in #2 above. Psychologist Albert Ellis, the originator of rational-emotive therapy, suggests the following:

    A. What rational support exists for your self-talk?
    B. What evidence exists to suggest your self-talk is exaggerated, distorted or inaccurate?
    C. What's the worst thing that could happen if things don't turn out the way you'd like?
    D. What positive things might occur if things don't turn out the way you'd like?

5. Replace your distress-maintaining thoughts *with self-soothing or self-validating thoughts* such as the following examples: *"I may feel upset now, but I'm proud of the progress we've already made."* *"As long as we take baby steps,*

expanding our boundaries is exciting, not scary." "My lover isn't perfect, and neither am I. We're both making honest efforts."

Making your own self-soothing relaxation tape: One of the most interesting ways to both relax yourself and highlight your capacity for self-soothing is to make your own audio recording. (Once again, I've adapted some ideas from the Davis, Eshelman & McKay *Relaxation and Stress Reduction Workbook.*)

Creating your own tape allows you to integrate just those relaxation approaches and self-soothing statements that work the best for you. It also allows you to pick your favorite, most soothing background music or sounds. Most people find New Age or classical selections (consider Debussy) especially nice. You'll need two tape decks if you do this, and need to do a bit of experimenting. I've personally found it works best to play my musical selection (David Lynch's *Sky of Mind*) on my good stereo and record the blank tape on my humbler stereo.

A relaxation script that describes deep breathing, deep muscle relaxation, or a mixture of both is a good way to begin your tape. It's also nice to describe a special place where you feel serene, calm and secure (for example, a beautiful beach, a mountain retreat, or even an indoor setting). When you describe it, bring in all of the senses you can — sight, hearing, touch, smell and taste. The more senses you engage, the more vivid your images will be.

You'll probably find it easier to write out what you want to say before recording. Once you've completed your relaxation section and moved into self-soothing images and self-validating statements, be sure to phrase them positively, for example, *As you imagine modeling for your lover, focus on feeling proud of your body, moving it in undulating, erotic ways and flirting with your eyes...* NOT *as you imagine... focus on not worrying about your stomach...*

Do some "dry run" experimenting with your voice before attempting your first "take." Practice keeping your voice relatively monotone, soothing and slow (remember, this is a *re-lax-a-tion* tape!). It might take up to a week to play around with the words and images you select, sound quality, and your delivery before you've created a "good enough" fifteen to twenty minute tape.

Then, lie down or sit comfortably and listen to your tape once or twice a day. As circumstances change or you get new ideas, periodically make new tapes for yourself. (*Tip: Be sure to "self-soothe" while making your own tape* — let go of perfectionism!)

Of course, you may have little interest in making your own tape. There are many helpful relaxation tapes available today from both catalogs and bookstores. The basic motto is: Whatever works, use it!

Giving yourself a self-soothing hug: One classic yoga position is a self-hug. Wrap your arms around yourself and hold the pose for awhile. You can gently press into your back with your fingers, or do whatever feels best to you. This is a stretch that helps you to relax your back and shoulders. It is also an expression of self-appreciation and self-love.

If you prefer, you can stroke any part of your body that helps calm and soothe you. Try stroking your neck down to the center of your chest, or using one hand to stroke your other arm. You can even do this while driving!

REPETITION. None of the *Love Skills* exercises or suggestions may be easy the first time you try. Don't be discouraged! Relax and try it again another time (not immediately after). Some of these activities, like so many good things in life, take practice before they come easily to you and before gaining the improvements you're looking for in your relationship. Stay focused on enhancement and enrichment, not perfection!

MAKING CHANGE IN YOUR RELATIONSHIP. The *Love Skills* approach is designed to gradually introduce positive change and growth in your sexual relationship. It encourages you to usher in new, more fulfilling ways of connecting and to let go of less satisfying old ways. But replacing old habits and patterns with new ones does involve a loss — you're giving up old ways. It can also be intimidating. You may feel awkward and unsure of yourself during an exercise. An exercise may bring up some old feelings from an earlier relationship, or even from childhood. Or you may be quite eager to try an exercise but your lover is reluctant — or the reverse. Or the benefits of the exercise may not show up for a while.

Any of these reactions may be uncomfortable enough to cause you to doubt the value of the activity, or perhaps even to doubt yourself.

All of these are common resistances to change, even positive change. Psychologists sometimes refer to this as the 90/10 rule. This means that you're 90% interested in enriching and improving your situation, but you're 10% resistant to change — you feel safer and more comfortable with the *known*, even when it isn't particularly satisfying, than with venturing into the *unknown*. If you're in a relationship in which only one of you is resistant, psychologists are quick to point out that the reluctant person is simply "carrying the resistance" for both of you. In other words, avoid finger-pointing.

Here are a couple of suggestions for breaking through your resistance to doing *Love Skills* exercises:

Listing Payoffs for Maintaining the Status Quo: To break through your resistances as an individual or as a couple, each of you can make a list of the "payoffs" for keeping things just as they are. The results are typically illuminating. Your list may range from "If I don't even try, I won't run any risk of failure" to "If he learns to give me oral sex, maybe he'll want to give it to others, as well." If your list is typical, it will contain a variety of distress-maintaining thoughts that you can address. The idea on pages 202-204, "*Replacing distress-maintaining self-talk with self-soothing self-talk*," coupled with any of the relaxation exercises, can be very helpful.

Getting Professional Help: Finally, for some couples, professional assistance in acquiring *Love Skills* can be a very beneficial experience and an appropriate solution to overcoming resistances. If you wish to pursue this avenue, refer to the *Resources for Lovers* section for organizations that can give you the names of qualified professionals in your area, or contact your local city or county psychological association.

Good Luck and Good Loving!

Glossary

Aerobic [air-OH-beak] Requiring oxygen. Regarding exercise, those forms of exercise requiring increased oxygen levels in the bloodstream and which, in moderation, enhance cardiovascular health.

Affectionate LoveTouch Any touch, from holding hands to snuggling, that communicates warmth, caring, support, reassurance and connection between lovers.

Anaerobic [ANN-air-O-beak] Not requiring oxygen. Regarding exercise, those forms of exercise that may build muscle or increase flexibility but do not require elevated levels of oxygen in the bloodstream or increased cardiovascular effort.

Anal sex Insertion of the penis into the rectum of a receiving lover.

Aphrodisiac [Af-row-DIZ-e-ak] A substance that increases, or is believed to increase, a person's sexual desire or capacity.

BodyLove The ability to love, accept and enjoy your body and that of your lover.

Clitoral [KLIH-toh-ral] glans The rounded tip of the clitoris, barely visible from under the clitoral hood.

Clitoral hood The fold of skin, counterpart to the foreskin of the penis, which covers the glans of the clitoris unless retracted to expose it.

Clitoris [KLIH-toh-ris] (Clit) The highly erotic structure of female genitals that develops from the same embryonic tissue as the male penis. The glans and hood are visible at the upper end of the labia minora, above the urethral opening. Its shaft and base extend into the body. The clitoris functions exclusively as a source of sexual pleasure.

Corona [koh-ROH-na] The sensitive rim of the glans penis.

Creative LovePlay Nonroutine creative or playful sexual experiences with a lover that can occur spontaneously or can be planned.

Cunnilingus [kun-nih-LING-gus] Oral stimulation of the vulva.

Daring LovePlay Sexually creative or playful activities a person is ready to explore that extend beyond his or her previous erotic boundaries.

Dildo [DILL-doe] A penis-shaped device used for sexual stimulation.

Door-opening phrases Verbal phrases that encourage lovers to share with each other their wants and feelings. Beginning phrases such as *Tell me...* or *Something I'm curious about...* facilitate dialog, as do open-ended questions such as *What sexual activities would you like to try?*

Ejaculation [e-JAK-you-lay-shun] The reflex release of semen through the urethra of the penis.

Erotica Explicit, sexually arousing material that is acceptable to the viewer or reader and is not degrading to men, women or children.

Fellatio [fel-A-she-o or show] Oral stimulation of the penis.

Flooding Feeling overwhelmed with negative reactions during vertical LoveTalk with a lover; feeling swamped with distress. Flooding is typically triggered by internal, distress-maintaining thoughts either of righteous indignation or of innocent victimhood. University research reveals men flood far more readily than women. (See physiologic flooding)

Foreskin The loose folds of skin covering the glans (tip) of the penis. Easily drawn back from the glans, it automatically retracts when the penis is erect, fully exposing the glans. It is often removed surgically by circumcision.

Frenulum [FREN-yoo-lum] The inverted "V," thin strip of skin connecting the glans to the shaft on the underside of the penis. It is present regardless of circumcision status.

Glans The head of the penis or clitoris, richly endowed with nerve endings.

"Gräfenberg" spot [GRAY-fen-berg] ("G" spot) A mass of erectile and glandular tissue that may surround the urethra just below the neck of the bladder. It is accessed through the vagina's anterior wall, about an inch or two inside. For some women, stimulation of "G" spot tissue produces intense sexual pleasure and triggers orgasm.

Horizontal LoveTalk Verbal expressions of desire and degree of satisfaction shared during sexual activity with a lover to enhance the erotic experience.

Kama Sutra honey dust powder A fragrantly scented, edible powder named after the *Kama Sutra*, a famous Indian sex manual. Available from catalogs or stores specializing in erotica.

Labia majora [LAY-bee-ah ma-JOR-ah] The outer, hair-covered lips enclosing the inner lips and clitoris.

Labia minora [LAY-bee-ah mih-NOR-ah] Also known as minor lips or inner lips, the hairless lips on each side of the vaginal opening that extend up to the clitoris.

LovePlay The ability to be creative, playful — and occasionally sexually naughty — in or out of bed.

LoveTalk The ability to communicate about sexual matters, both out of and in bed.

LoveTouch The ability to give and receive affirmation through touch.

Missionary position The "man above-woman below" sexual position named after the erroneous belief that early missionaries imposed it on natives. It is the most common position used in the United States, but not throughout the world.

Mons veneris [Moans veh-NEAR-is] Literally Latin for "mountain of Venus," the triangular mound of fatty tissue over the female pubic bone that is covered with pubic hair.

Orgasm The brief, intense culmination of sexual sensations throughout the body, accompanied by rhythmic muscular contractions in the genital area. For most, the physiologic release of tension is quickly followed by a sense of relaxation and well-being.

Perineum [Pear-eh-KNEE-um]; (Perineal [Pear-eh-KNEE-al] area) The thin, erotically sensitive tissue between the scrotal sac and anal opening of males, and between the lower end of the inner lips and anal opening of females.

Pheromones [FARE-oh-moans] Scents produced by the body that are often sexual attractants.

Physiologic flooding The physiologic arousal of the nervous system that accompanies flooding (increased heart rate, blood pressure, and often, trouble breathing) that interferes with listening constructively during LoveTalk. States of physiologic flooding and physiologic calm are opposites. (See also flooding)

Pornography Visual or written depictions of sexual behavior designed to evoke sexual excitement. The term is typically reserved for material that is perceived as degrading or violent.

Royal Treatment The special treatment one lover provides to the other, typically with advance planning, to acknowledge, pamper and show appreciation.

Scrotal Sac [SKROH-tal sak] The thin, loose sac of skin that contains the testes and has a layer of muscle fibers that contract involuntarily.

Semen [SEE-men] (Seminal [SEM-uh-nul] fluid) A viscous, alkaline fluid ejaculated through the penile urethra that contains sperm and fluids from the seminal vesicles and prostate.

Sensual Lovetouch Caressive, light touching of all areas of a lover's body that is not goal focused, but moment-to-moment sensation focused.

Sexual LoveTouch Touch more specifically focused on the genital area, or other parts of the body, that is designed to evoke the physiologic changes associated with sexual arousal and orgasm.

Stonewalling Ceasing to respond during Lovetalk; resorting to mumbling, stony silence, changing the subject, or other forms of distancing. A much higher percentage of stonewallers are men (85%) than women (15%), according to recent University research.

Urethra [you-REE-thrah] The duct (tube) through which urine and ejaculate leave the body. The female urethra is much shorter than the male urethra, contributing to the higher incidence of bladder infections in females.

Vagina [Va-JYE-nuh] The internal female muscular tube, about four inches long, extending from the vulva to the cervix, that serves as the birth canal and exit for menstrual flow. It is sexually sensitive, particularly in the lower portion, when stimulated by a penis, fingers, or a dildo.

Vaginal lips See labia majora and labia minora.

Vasocongestion [VAY-zoh-con-jest-shun] The extensive dilation of blood vessels in both deep and superficial body tissues in response to sexual stimulation.

Vertical LoveTalk The constructive "out-of-bed" language used to express thoughts, feelings and desires about the sexual aspects of a relationship.

Vibrator A battery operated or plug-in electrical device used for sexual stimulation. Battery operated vibrators are usually dildo-shaped; plug-in types come in an assortment of designs and are often purchased in department stores as "massagers."

Vulva [VUL vuh] The collective term for female external sex organs, including the mons, vaginal lips, clitoris, and vaginal opening.

Suggested Reading

Non-fiction About Relationships, Lovemaking and Sex

Barbach, L. (1994). *The Erotic Edge*. New York: E. P. Dutton.

Berkowitz, B. (1995). *What Men Won't Tell You but Women Need to Know*. New York: Avon Books.

Cash, T. (1991). *Body Image Therapy: A Program for Self-directed Change*. New York: Guilford. (This is actually a set of four audio cassettes with an eight page clinician's manual and twenty-nine page client workbook. Written by a psychologist at Old Dominion University well known for his research on body image.)

Comfort, A. (1991). *The New Joy of Sex*. New York: Pocket Books. (An updated version of a classic in the field.)

Davis, M., Eshelman, E. & McKay, M. (1995). *The Relaxation & Stress Reduction Workbook* (4th Ed.). Oakland, CA: New Harbinger Publications Inc.

Dodson, B. (1987). *Sex for One: The Joy of Selfloving*. New York: Crown Trade Paperbacks. (A very sex positive book introducing both sexes to self-stimulation, with the emphasis on women.)

Emmons, M. & Alberti, R. (1991). *Accepting Each Other: Individuality and Intimacy in Your Loving Relationship*. San Luis Obispo, CA: Impact Publishers.

Freedman, R. (1990). *Bodylove: Learning to Like our Looks and Ourselves.* New York: Harper & Row. (A practical guide offering specific exercises to women for relating more compassionately to their bodies.)

Friday, N. (1991). *Women on Top.* New York: Pocket Books. (Presents intriguing transcripts of diverse female fantasies. You can skip over the less helpful editorializing.)

Gottman, J. (1995). *Why Marriages Succeed or Fail.* New York: Simon & Schuster. (Presents the pioneering work of Gottman and his associates, highlighting both successful communication styles and negative communication patterns that are highly predictive of marital success or failure.)

Heiman, J. & Lo Piccolo, J. (1988). *Becoming Orgasmic: A Sexual Growth Program for Women.* Englewood Cliffs, NJ: Prentice-Hall. (The best of the self-help books designed to teach women how to reach orgasm and heighten their sexual experience alone or with a partner.)

LaCroix, N. (1989). *Sensual Massage.* New York: Henry Holt. (A book providing excellent photography and clear instructions for giving and receiving sensual massage.)

McCarthy, B. & McCarthy, E. (1993). *Sexual Awareness.* New York: Carroll & Graf.

McCarthy, B. & McCarthy, E. (1989). *Female Sexual Awareness: Achieving Sexual Fulfillment.* New York: Carroll & Graf.

Michael, R., Gagnon, J., Laumann, E. & Kolata, G. (1994). *Sex in America.* Boston: Little, Brown. (The most comprehensive survey of what we do sexually to date.)

Montagu, A. (1986). *Touching: The Human Significance of the Skin.* New York: Harper & Row.

Morin, J. (1996). *The Erotic Mind: Unlocking the Inner Sources of Sexual Passion and Fulfillment.* New York: HarperCollins.

Ogden, G. (1994). *Women Who Love Sex.* New York: Pocket Books.

Stoppard, M. (1991). *The Magic of Sex*. New York: Dorling Kindersley. (Written by a physician who includes material on reproduction, contraception and sexually transmitted disease.)

Stubbs, R. (1989). *Erotic Massage: The Touch of Love*. Larkspur, CA: Secret Garden. (Thoughtful, specific suggestions for sensual touching.)

Tessina, T. (1988). *Gay Relationships: How to Find Them, How to Improve Them, How to Make Them Last*. Los Angeles: Tarcher. (This is an extremely practical guidebook that assists gays and lesbians in the whole range of activities, from coming out to family and friends to developing relationship skills.)

Zilbergeld, B. (1992). *The New Male Sexuality*. New York: Bantam. (This update of the most popular book on male sexuality in the 1980's helps both men and women overcome untenable sexual attitudes and stereotypes through insight and exercises.)

Resources for Lovers

Erotic Reading Material

Fanny Hill

Lady Chatterly's Lover

Lolita

Madame Bovary

Man with a Maid

My Secret Life

The Pearl

Sleeping Beauty (series)

Tropic of Cancer

"Mainstream" Films with erotic themes or scenes (listed in alphabetical order

About Last Night Demi Moore; Rob Lowe

American Gigolo Richard Gere; Lauren Hutton

Body Heat William Hurt; Kathleen Turner

Bull Durham Susan Sarandon; Tim Robbins; Kevin Costner

Cousin, Cousine Marie-Christine Barrault; Victor Lanoux

Exit to Eden Dana Delaney; Rosie O'Donnell

Fabulous Baker Boys Michelle Pfeiffer; Jeff Bridges; Beau Bridges

The Hunger Catherine Deneuve; David Bowie

An Officer and a Gentleman Deborah Winger; Richard Gere

The Piano Holly Hunter; Harvey Keitel

Red Shoe Diaries David Duchovny (Showtime anthology series)

Romancing the Stone Kathleen Turner; Michael Douglas

sex, lies and videotape Andie McDowell; James Spader

Summer Lovers Peter Gallagher; Daryl Hannah

The Truth about Cats and Dogs Jeanine Garafalo; Uma Thurman

Threesome Steven Baldwin; Laura Doyle

White Palace Susan Sarandon; James Spader

Erotic Videos

Featured in *Time*, "48 Hours," etc., Femme Distribution, Inc. 1-800-456-LOVE to order catalog. Most of these films run about seventy minutes and emphasize female fantasies and sensibilities. There are two versions of the tapes, both an explicit and a non explicit version.

The Sinclaire Institute
P.O. Box 8865
Chapel Hill, NC 27515
1-800-955-0888 (24 hours, daily)
(Produces and distributes educational videos on sexual
interaction between couples. Most tapes are ninety minutes long
and feature one M.D. and one sex therapist who provide
"voice-over" advice during explicit portions of the videos.)

Massage Tables
Love Table
BodyCare Products
San Diego, CA
(619) 465-5566.
Massage table uniquely designed for comfortable massage and a
wide variety of sexual positions.

Sex Toys (both of the following have catalogs)

Eve's Garden	Good Vibrations
119 West 57th Street	1210 Valencia Street
New York, New York 10019	San Francisco, CA 94110
1-800-848-3837	Mail order 1 -800-289-8423

Professional Organizations
American Association of Sex Educators, Counselors, and
  Therapists (AASECT)
Howard Ruppel, Ph.D., Executive Director
608 5th Avenue
Mt. Vernon, IA 52314
Phone: (319) 897-8407
(Can provide referrals to AASECT certified sex therapists in your area.)

American Board of Sexology
1929 18th Street, NW, Suite 1166
Washington, D.C. 20009
1-800-533-3521
(Can provide referrals to Diplomates and Clinical Supervisors in
your area.)

Gay, Lesbian and Gender Issues
National Gay and Task force
1517 U Street NW
Washington, D.C.
(202) 332-7483
(Referrals and political action in support of gay/les/bi concerns.)

International Foundation of Gender Education
P.O. Box 229
Waltham, MA 02254-0229
(Education, referrals, research into crossdressing, transsexualism
and other "transgender" behavior.)

Society for the Scientific Study of Sexuality
Howard Ruppel, Ph.D., Executive Director
P.O. Box 208
Mt. Vernon, IA 52314
Phone: (same as AASECT)
(Holds annual conventions and publishes *The Journal of Sex
Research.*)

Sexually Transmitted Disease (STD) Information
Centers for Disease Control
Public Health Service AIDS Hotlines
(800) 342-AIDS, 24 hours a day, 7 days a week.
Spanish speakers may call (800) 344-7432, daily from 8:00 a.m. -
2:00 a.m. (EST). For the hearing impaired, call (800) 243-7889,
Monday through Friday from 10:00 a.m to 10:00 p.m. (EST) .

STD National Hotline (Centers for Disease Control)
(800) 227-8922, 8:00 a.m. - 11:00 p.m. (EST) weekdays.
Provides information about STD's and referrals to STD clinics.

Hepatitis Hotline (Centers for Disease Control)
(404) 332-4555
Provides information by phone or fax on modes of transmission,
prevention and statistics regarding all forms of viral hepatitis.

The Herpes Resource Center
ASHA, Dept. PR 46
P.O. Box 13827
Research Triangle Park
North Carolina 27709
(800) 230-6039
Provides a quarterly journal with up-to-date information about herpes and referral to local support groups and counseling. (Send $1.00 for information or call the 800 number.)

A Note from the Author
If you have benefited from my book and would like to extend our relationship, please contact me at the address below. I am available for Love Skills seminars, lectures, and private consultation. Audio and videotaped material will also be available to assist you in continuing your Love Skills journey.

Linda De Villers, Ph.D.
Love Skills
P.O. Box 3166
Manhattan Beach, California 90266-1166

For more information about ordering copies of this book, or for permission to reproduce any material from *Love Skills* for any purpose, please contact my publisher:

Impact Publishers, Inc.
P.O. Box 1094
San Luis Obispo California 93406-1094

IMPACT PUBLISHERS
"STATEMENT ON SAFER SEX"

The management, authors, and editorial advisors of Impact Publishers, Inc. — predominantly professionals in the human services — recognize safe and healthy approaches to sexual expression as one of the principal health and social issues of our time. We offer the following statement for your serious consideration:

• Sexual expression is a basic, normal, positive, intensely personal and highly satisfying human activity. Although sexual practices are often publicly regulated by social mores, religious values, and law, individuals and couples decide privately whether or not to follow such regulations.

• Responsible sexual practice requires good information, including knowledge of the fundamentals of human sexuality, responsible family planning, contraceptive choices, and protection against sexually transmitted diseases.

• Sexually transmitted diseases, such as Acquired Immune Deficiency Syndrome (AIDS), various forms of Herpes, Hepatitis B, and the several Venereal Diseases, are serious and widespread public health problems, both in the United States and throughout the populated world.

• Safer sex — minimizing the risks of sexually transmitted diseases — includes at minimum the following:

- an absolutely certain, long-term, exclusively monogamous relationship, *or ALL of the following:*

- regular periodic physical examinations;

- conscientious unfailing use of condoms (preferably with spermicides) during intercourse;

- awareness and avoidance of common risk factors in STD's (e.g., intravenous drug use, high-risk populations);

- honest and open discussion of sexual habits and preferences with potential partners;

- infrequent changing of partners.

• Each individual — married or single — has the right to freedom of choice in sexual expression, so long as the practice involves consenting adults and consciously avoids physical or psychological harm to any person.

• No one is obligated to have a sexual relationship with another person — including a marriage partner — unless he or she wishes to do so.

• The following AIDS facts are reproduced from the brochure, *Understanding AIDS: A Message from the Surgeon General*, released in 1988 by C. Everett Koop, M.D., then Surgeon General of the United States:

- *The AIDS virus may live in the human body for years before actual symptoms appear.*

- *Who you are has nothing to do with whether you are in danger of being infected with the AIDS virus. What matters is what you do.*

- *There are two main ways you can get AIDS. First, you can become infected by having sex — oral, anal, or vaginal — with someone who is infected with the AIDS virus. Second, you can be infected by sharing drug needles and syringes with an infected person.*

- *Your chances of coming into contact with the virus increase with the number of sex partners you have.*

- *You won't get AIDS through everyday contact... a mosquito bite... saliva, sweat, tears, urine, or a bowel movement... a kiss... clothes, a telephone, or from a toilet seat.*

- *A person can be infected with the AIDS virus without showing any symptoms at all.*

- *Condoms are the best preventive measure against AIDS besides not having sex and practicing safe behavior.*

- *RISKY BEHAVIOR*
Sharing drug needles and syringes.
Anal sex, with or without a condom.
Vaginal or oral sex with someone who shoots drugs or engages in anal sex.
Sex with someone you don't know well (a pickup or prostitute) or with someone you know has several sex partners.
Unprotected sex (without a condom) with an infected person.

- *SAFE BEHAVIOR*
Not having sex.
Sex with one mutually faithful, uninfected partner.
Not shooting drugs.
- *If you know someone well enough to have sex, then you should be able to talk about AIDS. If someone is unwilling to talk, you shouldn't have sex.*

Index

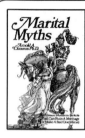